Insider Guide

Ace Your Case® V:
Return to the
Case Interview

WetFeet®

Helping you make smarter career decisions.

WetFeet, Inc.

The Folger Building

101 Howard Street

Suite 300

San Francisco, CA 94105

Phone: (415) 284-7900 or 1-800-926-4JOB

Fax: (415) 284-7910

Website: www.WetFeet.com

Ace Your Case® V: Return to the Case Interview

ISBN: 1-58207-444-5

Table of Contents

Nailing the Case 55

Case-by-Case Rules at a Glance

Here's a summary of the different types of cases you'll find in this Insider Guide, along with some rules that should help you ace your answer.

Market-Sizing Questions

- Use round numbers.
- Show your work.
- Use paper and calculator.

Business Operations Questions

- Isolate the main issue.
- Apply a framework.
- Think "action."

Business Strategy Questions

- Think frameworks.
- Ask questions.
- Work from big to small.

Resume Questions

- Know your story.
- Keep the Parent Test in mind.
- Let your excitement shine!

The Interview Unplugged

- Overview

- The Case Interview

Overview

When it comes to preparing for your case interviews, there's one word and one word only: practice. By now, you're spending all of your spare time thinking about why Google is getting into e-mail, why customer service jobs are moving to India, and how much mustard is consumed in Idaho. Your family thinks you're an oddball, but you're on the right track. You're probably even starting to enjoy thinking about these issues. Watch out: You might be turning into a consultant.

This guide is designed to be a companion volume to *Ace Your Case!*, *Ace Your Case II*, *Ace Your Case III*, and *Ace Your Case IV*. It offers a brand new set of case questions and answers accompanied by new detailed explanations about the different case types. Many of our sample case questions are based on real, live case questions that people received in their interviews last year.

For those who haven't seen our other case-interviewing guides, *Ace Your Case!* discusses the consulting interview in general and offers a primer containing a number of common frameworks and B-school–type tools (watch out for the 4Cs and the 4Ps, not to mention the infamous Five Forces) that should help you attack your case questions. *Ace Your Case II, Ace Your Case III,* and *Ace Your Case IV* each contain 15 specific case questions and detailed recommended answers, as does this edition.

A word about how to use this guide: We strongly recommend that you try to solve the questions first, without looking at the answers. After you've given them your best shot, go ahead and check out our recommended answers. If you find that our "good answer" differs from yours, see whether there's something you can learn from our suggestions. But don't panic—there are usually numerous ways to answer any case question. It's far more important to note the approach, as well as the interviewer's likely responses, which obviously won't be included in your own answers. As you sharpen those skills, keep thinking to yourself, "I love these case questions!" Pretty soon you'll find yourself talking like a consultant!

 Insider Tip

Keep the firm's reputation and areas of strength in mind as you launch into your case answer. Firms that are known for a particular type of work are likely to be more sensitive to those issues in the case questions they give.

The Case Interview

Background

Many management consulting firms, especially the strategy firms (McKinsey, Boston Consulting Group, Bain, Mercer, et al.) love to give prospective employees a problem to solve during the course of the interview. These problem-solving exercises, known generally as "case questions," are designed to help the interviewer screen candidates and determine which people really have what it takes to be a real, live, card-carrying management consultant.

Case questions come in many forms and levels of complexity. To help you get a handle on them, we have identified four different categories of questions:

- Market-sizing questions
- Business operations questions
- Business strategy questions
- Resume questions

(Note that we are not covering the brainteaser category in this Insider Guide. Consulting firms rarely ask brainteaser questions; other types of cases give much more insight into the type of thinking that makes a good consultant.)

Each of these prototypes has certain distinguishing features, which we discuss below. In addition, our insiders recommend certain "rules of the road" that should help you successfully navigate the different types of questions. Don't worry—you'll never be asked to spit out a category name and serial number for the questions you receive in the interview. Nevertheless, if you can identify the type of question, you will have a better idea about how to effectively attack the problem.

What Your Interviewer Is Seeking

It may seem as if your interviewer is using the case technique for one purpose alone: to humiliate prospective consultants. Although a few interviewers do seem to take a perverse pleasure in watching candidates writhe, this isn't the true goal of the technique. According to insiders, case questions really do help interviewers evaluate a candidate's aptitude for consulting. What does that mean exactly? Whether you're an undergrad, an MBA, or a PhD, consulting interviewers will likely depend on the case questions to check you out on the following dimensions:

- Analytical ability
- Structured thinking
- Intelligence
- Ability to not break into hives under pressure
- Common sense
- Ability to think on your feet
- Interest in problem solving
- Business intuition
- Facility with numbers
- Presentation skills
- Communication skills
- Ability to sort through information and focus on the key points
- Ability to analyze and then make recommendations based on the analysis
- Creativity
- Enthusiasm

Before you bid all your points to get an interview with name-your-consulting-firm, we recommend that you spend some time thinking about how consulting fits you. In particular, you must have good answers to two questions:

• Why do you want to be a consultant?
• And why do you want to work for this firm?

If you have good answers to these two questions, then you're ready to start thinking about cases. We start by discussing the case interview as it relates to several categories of candidates: undergraduates, MBAs, advanced-degree candidates, and experienced hires.

Undergraduates

Consulting interviewers tell us that the case questions and the expected answers for undergraduates tend to be simpler and more understandable than those for MBA students. Market-sizing questions are very popular (you will almost certainly get at least one of these), as are general business strategy problems. In the business strategy area, the companies and the topics may also seem a little friendlier; you're more likely to get a case about a beer company than about a company trying to license the latest packet-filtering technology for data encryption. Operations questions (with the exception of the ever-popular declining-profits question) are less common for undergraduates, and resume questions will more likely focus on academic or extracurricular activities than on work experiences.

Interviewers say that they often provide more prompting to undergraduate candidates during the interview. In evaluating your answer to a question, only the most sadistic interviewer would expect you to regurgitate all of the standard business-school terminology and techniques (after all, how else could the company justify paying MBAs the big bucks?). But beware: Rank amateurs are definitely not welcome. Thus, you must have a general understanding of basic business relationships (e.g., revenues – costs = profits), but don't get your knickers in a knot if you can't name even one of the Five Forces.

Here are a few real, live case questions fielded by our undergraduate customers:

- How many jelly beans would it take to fill a 747?

- Your client is the owner of a hip sushi restaurant and bar in New York. The place is always packed, but it isn't profitable. What's going on?

- Two prominent hospitals are planning a merger. What are some of the issues they should think about?

MBAs

MBAs have long been the heavy hitters of the consulting workforce. As a result, the case interview reaches its most sophisticated and demanding form in the MBA interview. All types of questions—from the simple market-sizer to the gnarliest of business strategy problems—are fair game. Practically any industry or functional issue area is possible material for the case question. An MBA candidate will be expected to be familiar with a number of the standard MBA frameworks and concepts. Also, the case will possibly have a few tricky twists or turns. For example, what might seem like a pure and simple international strategy question might be complicated by an unexpected restriction related to the European regulatory environment.

Interviewers tell us that most MBAs have a polished interview technique and understand the basics of many case problems. Therefore, they look for depth in the answer (what they describe as an ability to peel the onion and a real familiarity with business concepts). We understand that at least some recruiters like to ask resume case questions because they provide an opportunity to get more detail about the candidate's background and problem-solving experiences.

Here are a few real, live case questions fielded by our MBA customers:

- How many diapers are sold in the United States in a year?

- An online brokerage is contemplating expansion into additional financial services categories. Should it go ahead with the expansion?

- A sunglasses manufacturer discovers that its costs are far above industry average. What should it do?

Other Advanced-Degree Candidates

Although consulting firms are attracting record numbers of MBA applicants, several of the top firms have started to look beyond traditional feeder programs to identify top talent. According to WetFeet customers and recruiters, the different firms have very different approaches to advanced-degree candidates. McKinsey and BCG, among others, have launched aggressive recruiting programs aimed at PhDs, MDs, JDs, and others at the top schools. In the process, some of these firms have created customized recruiting and training programs for advanced-degree candidates. Other firms continue to consider advanced-degree candidates on a case-by-case basis, often pitting them against undergraduate or MBA candidates, depending on their background.

If you enter a separate recruiting track, you will, according to our customers, still have to contend with interviews that are similar in format to that of undergraduate and MBA recruiting programs. In other words, expect a heavy dose of case interview questions along with the general get-to-know-you queries. One slight difference is that, in addition to seeing whether you can handle the substance of the case question, the recruiter will also be looking to see "if [you] can break out of the PhD box." In other words, can you adapt to the real world and answer questions without giving too much detail?

According to WetFeet customers, case questions for advanced-degree candidates usually don't require you to carry your own MBA toolbox. Instead, the questions may relate to previous research (your resume is usually a font of material), or they may resemble undergraduate case studies that check a person's intuition, common sense, analytical skills, and problem-solving abilities. Interviewers at various top firms say they may be more inclined to prompt candidates with questions, and they may be satisfied with a good, solid analytical answer that doesn't necessarily incorporate all of the latest business buzzwords.

Check out these case questions fielded by our advanced-degree customers:

- How many taxicabs are there in New York City?
- A winery has hired you to tell it why it has been experiencing declining profits.
- Question for someone who studied physics: What has been the most important development in the field of physics in the last five years?

Experienced Hires

If you are seeking to join a consulting firm from industry, or from another consulting firm, your interviewing experience may differ from that described in this report. According to WetFeet customers, experienced-hire candidates may or may not face a battery of case questions. There is no hard-and-fast rule, but it seems as though people with more experience (10-plus years) and people who have already worked for a name-brand consulting firm are relatively unlikely to face a case as part of their review process. In contrast, people who have worked in industry for a few years and who are seeking to enter at a middle level are likely to go through a process similar to that used for MBAs (i.e., expect lots of cases). In particular, if you are changing careers (e.g., moving from nonprofit work to consulting) and not signing on as an industry authority, you'll probably be scrutinized for your consulting aptitude—as demonstrated by your ability to field case questions.

Typical case questions faced by our experienced-hire customers include:

- Your client is a struggling telecom firm. How would you turn it around?

- Your client is a U.S.-based company that sells telephones by mail. Mail sales of telephones are a small portion of the company's overall business, and sales are below average for mail-order sales of appliances. Should the client continue to sell phones in this way? If so, how should it make the operation more profitable?

- Specific questions related to their area of expertise.

Company-Specific Variations

As you enter the ring with consultants from a variety of firms, you'll probably notice differences in the questions you receive, as well as the style and approach of the case interview. More often than not, these differences arise from the differences in the personalities and experiences of your interviewers. However, several firms have developed their own approach to the case interview. One variation involves giving a candidate a written case before the interview and asking him to prepare to discuss the case in detail during the interview. We understand that IBM Global Services (formerly PricewaterhouseCoopers) and Monitor Group have given preprinted cases to candidates before an interview. Monitor has also used a group interview technique that requires competing candidates to work with each other to solve a problem, while McKinsey has been experimenting with a process for undergraduates that includes both a written case test and a group interview.

One other thing to keep in mind: Recruiters suggest that you would be wise to keep the firm's reputation and areas of strength in mind as you launch into your case answer. Firms that are known for a particular type of work are likely to be more sensitive to those issues in the case questions they give. For example, if you're interviewing with Towers Perrin, you shouldn't be surprised to find a "people issue" somewhere in the case. If you're talking with Deloitte Consulting, keep "operations" in mind as you craft an answer—and don't talk about how it's important to work only with the company's top management. And, if you're interviewing with Bain, remember how much importance the company attaches to "measurable results" and "data-driven" analysis.

Case-by-Case Rules

- Market-Sizing Case

- Business Operations Cases

- Business Strategy Cases

- Resume Cases

Market-Sizing Cases

Case Rules

Overview

Consultants love to ask market-sizing questions. Not only are they easy to create, discuss, and evaluate, they are also highly representative of an important type of work done by consultants. In their simplest form, market-sizing cases require the candidate to determine the size of a particular market (hence the name). In the real world, this information can be especially helpful when gauging the attractiveness of a new market. In the interview context, a market-sizing question might be pitched in an extremely straightforward manner (e.g., "What is the market for surfboards in the United States?"). Or it may be disguised as a more complex question (e.g., "Do you think Fidelity should come out with a mutual fund targeted at high-net-worth individuals?") that requires the respondent to peel away the extraneous detail to identify the market-sizing issue at the core. In a more highly developed variation, the interviewer might ask a strategy or operations case question that requires the respondent to do some market-sizing in order to come up with an appropriate recommendation.

The Scorecard

Market-sizing questions allow the interviewer to test the candidate's facility with numbers, powers of analysis, and common sense. For example, if you were asked to size the surfboard market, you would need to make basic assumptions about the market. (How many people surf? How many boards does a typical surfer dude or gal own? How often will he or she get a new one? Are there other big purchasers besides individual surfers? Is there a market for used boards?) You would also need to make a few basic calculations (number of surfers **X** number of new boards per year + total quantity purchased by other types of customers, etc.). As you work through these issues, the interviewer would also get a glimpse of your common sense. (Did you assume that everybody in the U.S. population would be a potential surfer, or did you try to estimate the population in prime surfing areas like California and Hawaii?)

> " "
> **We get the 'deer in the headlights' look from time to time. That's an automatic ding.**

Location

Market-sizing questions can pop up in all interviews. They are almost certain to make an appearance in undergraduate and advanced-degree interviews. Indeed, both undergraduates and PhDs report receiving exactly the same market-sizing questions in their respective interviews. MBAs are also likely to receive market-sizing questions; however, a common and more complex variation typical of an MBA interview involves assessing the opportunity for a new product. For example, you might be asked whether your pharmaceutical company client should develop and market a drug for male pattern baldness. Part of the analysis would require you to estimate the market potential (i.e., market size) for the drug.

Mastering Your Market-Sizing Questions

Market-sizing questions can intimidate. But once you understand the rules (and practice your technique), you can come to view these cases as slow pitches right over the center of the plate. So, just how many golf balls are used in the United States in a year? You don't know, and the truth is, neither does your interviewer. In fact, your interviewer doesn't even care what the real number is. But remember, she does care about your ability to use logic, common sense, and creativity to get to a plausible answer. And she wants to make sure you don't turn tail when you've got a few numbers to run. Which brings us to the three rules for market-sizing questions.

Rule 1: Use Round Numbers

Even if you weren't a multivariate calculus stud, you can impress your interviewer with your number-crunching abilities if you stick to round numbers. They're much easier to add, subtract, multiply, and divide, and since we've already decided that the exact answer doesn't matter anyway, go ahead and pick something that you can toss around with ease. Good examples? One hundred, one million, ten dollars, two, one-half. The population of New York City? Ten million, give or take. The length of a standard piece of paper? Round 11 inches up to a foot.

Rule 2: Show Your Work

Case questions are the ultimate "show your work" questions. In fact, your exact answer matters less than the path you took to get there. Remember, the market-sizing question is merely a platform through which your interviewer can test your analysis, creativity, and comfort with numbers.

Rule 3: Use Paper and Calculator

If you feel more comfortable writing everything down and using a calculator, do! Most interviewers will not care if you use a pencil and paper to keep your thoughts organized and logical. And if pulling out the HP to multiply a few numbers keeps you from freaking out, then by all means do it. Your interviewer will be more impressed if you are calm, cool, and collected, so if using props helps you, then go for it.

Business Operations Cases

Overview

A fair number of case questions cover operations issues. Given the existing economic environment, the mix of consulting business has shifted more toward operations and process-focused cases, so be prepared for at least one of these types of questions. Broadly speaking, "operations" refers to everything that's involved in running a business and getting product out the door. In a manufacturing plant, this would include the purchasing and transporting of raw materials, the manufacturing processes, the scheduling of staff and facilities, the distribution of the product, the servicing of equipment in the field, and so on. In its broadest sense, operations would even include the sales and marketing of the company's products and the systems used to track sales. Whereas strategy questions deal with the future direction of the firm (e.g., whether to enter a new line of business), operations deals with the day-to-day running of the business. It is particularly fertile ground for consulting work, and for case questions. Some of the most typical case questions of this type are those that require the candidate to explain why a company's sales or profits have declined.

The Scorecard

Consultants like to ask operations questions because they allow the interviewer to see whether the candidate understands fundamental issues related to running a business (e.g., the relationship between revenues and costs, and the relationship and impact of fixed costs and variable costs on a company's profitability). In addition, operations questions require the candidate to demonstrate a good grasp of process and an ability to sort through a pile of information and identify the most important factors.

Location

Operations questions are fair game for all candidates, including undergraduates and advanced-degree candidates. According to our customers, the declining profits questions are some of the most popular types of cases around, and almost all candidates can expect to get at least one of these. That said, MBAs are typically expected to explore these questions in greater detail and have a better grasp of key business issues and terminology. MBAs could also get tossed more complicated operations questions. For example, an MBA case might involve understanding the implications of allocating fixed costs in a certain way, or, perhaps, the impact on the balance sheet of a certain type of financing.

Undergraduates and non-MBA candidates still need to be familiar with a few basic operational concepts, such as the relationship between costs and revenues, and the various things that might have an impact on them. In addition, under-graduates might expect the topic of the question to be more familiar. For example, an undergraduate might get lobbed a question about the implications of launching a new national chain of restaurants. An MBA might get a question about factors that would allow a manufacturing operation to increase throughput.

Optimizing Your Business Operations Answers

Operations case questions are more complex than market-sizing questions. Not only do they typically require basic business knowledge (or, at the very least, a good deal of common sense), but they also frequently require the candidate to think like a detective. For example, the interviewer might ask why an airline has been losing money while its market share has increased. There could be many reasons for this: Revenues might be down (and that, in turn, might be caused by any number of things, including ticket price wars, lower ridership, growing accounts payable, and so on); costs might be higher (due to higher fuel costs, greater landing fees, higher plane maintenance costs, and other factors); or the airline could be operating more inefficiently (e.g., higher passenger loads might require it to lease additional aircraft or pay staff overtime). In any case, a successful analysis of the question requires the candidate to think clearly and efficiently about the question. To help with these types of questions, here are some rules you'll want to keep in mind:

Rule 1: Isolate the Main Issue

Operations questions usually have lots of potential answers. The first step in identifying a good answer (and demonstrating your analytical firepower) is to separate the wheat from the chaff. Once you've zeroed in on the main issue, you'll be able to apply your energy to working out a good conclusion to the problem.

Rule 2: Apply a Framework

Frameworks were made for cracking operations questions. They will help you sift through lots of data and organize your answer. A useful framework can be something as simple as saying, "If the airline is losing money, it has something to do with either costs or revenues," and moving on to talk about each of these areas in turn.

Rule 3: Think Action!

Unlike your market-sizing question, operations questions never end with a nice, neat analysis. Rather, the goal here is action. The hypothetical client is usually facing a critical issue: Revenues are falling, costs are rising, production is crashing. Something needs to be done. As a consultant, you will be hired to give advice.

As a candidate, you should be sensitive to the fact that your analysis must drive toward a solution. Even if you need more data before you're able to make a final recommendation, you should acknowledge that you are evaluating various courses of action. Better yet, you should lay out a plan for next steps.

Business Strategy Cases

Overview

Business strategy cases are the granddaddies (and demons) of the case question world. Consultants love to use these questions because they touch on so many different issues. A good strategy question can have a market-sizing piece, a logic puzzle, multiple operations issues, and a major dose of creativity and action thrown in for good measure. Moreover, a complex strategy question can go in many different directions, thereby allowing the interviewer to probe the candidate's abilities in a variety of areas. Again, strategy case questions can run the gamut from a complex, multi-industry, multinational, multi-issue behemoth to a localized question with a pinpoint focus.

The Scorecard

Depending on the nature of the question, the interviewer can use it to assess anything and everything from your ability to handle numbers to your ability to wade through a mass of detailed information and synthesize it into a compelling business strategy. Of all the different types of case questions, these are also the most similar to the actual work you'll do on the job (at least at the strategy firms). One other thing the interviewer will be checking carefully: your presentation skills.

Location

Strategy case questions are fair game for any type of candidate. For undergraduates, they will often be more two-dimensional and straightforward. For MBA candidates, they frequently have several layers of issues, and perhaps an international or other twist to boot. Although most strategy boutiques will use this kind of case as a mainstay in their recruiting efforts, firms with more of an operations focus may rely more heavily on operations questions.

Simplifying the Strategy Stumpers

Because business strategy questions can involve many different elements, they may inspire fear in the weak of heart. Although it's true that strategy questions can be the most difficult, they can also be the most fun. This is your opportunity to play CEO, or at least advisor to the CEO. You can put all of your business intuition and your hard-nosed, data-driven research to work and come up with a plan that will bring a huge multinational corporation into the limelight—or not. Does it matter that you just crafted a story about why a credit-card company should go into the Italian market when your best friend who interviewed immediately prior to you recommended against going Italian? No, not really. Unless, of course, your friend did a better job of exploring the case question. What does that mean? By going through this book (and the other WetFeet *Ace Your Case* guides), you're already a step ahead of the game. However, here are the rules you'll want to keep in mind as you tackle your strategy case questions.

Rule 1: Think Frameworks

While analyzing a really juicy strategy question you might be able to draw information and jargon out of almost every course in your school's core business curriculum. Don't succumb to temptation! Your interviewer will be much more impressed by a clear and simple story about how you are attacking the question and where you are going with your analysis. The best way to do this is to apply a framework to the problem. As with operations questions, this means setting out a plan of attack up front and following it through to conclusion. One other big benefit: Having a clear framework will help you organize your analysis.

Rule 2: Ask Questions

Successful consulting is as much about asking the right questions as it is about providing a good answer. Likewise, your solution to a strategy case will be much better if you've focused your energy on the right issue. To help you get there, don't hesitate to ask your interviewer questions. In the best case, he may help you avoid a derailment; in the worst case, he'll understand your thought process as you plow through the analysis.

Rule 3: Work from Big to Small

Even though the strategy case you are examining was the subject of a study that lasted several months, you probably have about 15 minutes to provide your answer. Therefore it's essential that you start by looking at the most significant issues first. Besides, this is a great discipline for future consultants; the client may be paying for your time by the hour, so you'll want to make sure that you really are adding value.

Resume Cases

Overview

One favorite type of alternative case question is the resume case. Instead of cooking up a case question based on a carefully disguised project from his files, the interviewer will pull something straight from the candidate's resume. Usually, these cases stem from a previous professional experience, but occasionally you'll get something like: "I see you play rugby. Describe for me all of the different positions on a rugby team, and the play strategy for each." Frequently, the interviewer will ask the candidate to walk through a previous work project or experience and explain how he or she decided on a particular course of action. As the candidate goes through the discussion, the interviewer may then change a few critical assumptions and ask the candidate to explain how he or she would have responded. For example, if you had started and run a successful computer repair service, the interviewer might ask how you would have responded if a local computer store had created a knock-off service and offered it at a lower price.

The Scorecard

The resume case is a way for the interviewer to dig a little deeper into your resume and at the same time test your case-cracking capabilities. (It also adds a little variety to a grueling day of interviews.) Here, the interviewer is testing for your ability to communicate—in layman's terms—a topic that is very familiar to you. Resume cases are generally a good opportunity for you to toot your own horn a bit about your past experience and exude confidence, competence, and enthusiasm about things you really understand.

Location

The resume question is fair game for undergrads, MBAs, and advanced-degree candidates. Naturally, because the resumes for each type of candidate differ significantly, the types of questions also differ. MBAs can expect business-oriented questions; advanced-degree candidates can expect questions related to their previous research. PhD students tell us that they commonly receive resume cases. Not only do resume cases allow the candidate to avoid feeling like he or she has to master a whole new lexicon and body of frameworks, they test his or her communications skills.

Rocking Your Resume Cases

Because the resume case question takes the discussion to your home turf, there isn't really a secret recipe for pulling apart the question. Rather, the way to be successful here is to follow a few basic interview rules.

Rule 1: Know Your Story

Nothing will make you look worse—and help you find the door more quickly—than not knowing what you put on your own resume. Make sure you've reviewed all of the items on your resume before the interview. Write down a few notes about what you did at each job, and the main message you want to convey through each bullet point on your resume. Think up a short story for each bullet point that will provide compelling evidence to support those messages.

Rule 2: Keep the Parent Test in Mind

This is not the place to play the polyglot; nobody will be impressed with your ability to speak techno-babble. The interviewer will assume that you know everything there is to know about your area of expertise, whether that's molecular biology or your computer-repair service. The real question is can you tell others about what you did without sending them into a coma? It may sound easy, but many people seem incapable of communicating what they know. Our suggestion? Practice talking about your work as if you were telling your parents all about it.

Rule 3: Let Your Excitement Shine

This is your home field, so use it to your advantage. Talk about your past work with energy and enthusiasm. Believe it or not, even consultants like a little passion. Besides, if you're sitting there griping about a previous work experience, guess what's running through your interviewer's mind: "Whoa, Nelly. This cat could be trouble!"

The Practice Range

- Market-Sizing Questions

- Business Operations Questions

- Business Strategy Questions

- Resume Questions

Market-Sizing Questions

Remember the rules for market-sizing questions:

1. Use round numbers.

2. Show your work.

3. Use paper and calculator.

What is the total number of automobile tires sold in the United States each year?

Key questions to ask:

Total # of people × avg car ownership = total cars → ×4 = # tires $\quad$ 0.9

car tire life = 6 yrs., replace every 6 $\qquad$ 0.1 × 10

Basic equations/numbers:

How you'd track the numbers down:

CASE 2

What is the average equivalent number of cocoa beans that Hershey's buys each year for its entire U.S. chocolate bar business?

Key questions to ask:

Basic equations/numbers:

How you'd track the numbers down:

How many pages of paper would it take to completely encircle the earth at the equator?

Key questions to ask:

Basic equations/numbers:

How you'd track the numbers down:

How many pay phones are there in Manhattan?

Key questions to ask:

_____

_____

_____

_____

Basic equations/numbers:

_____

_____

_____

_____

How you'd track the numbers down:

_____

_____

_____

Business Operations Questions

Remember the rules for business operations questions:

1. Isolate the main issue.

2. Apply a framework.

3. Think action!

CASE 5

Your client is the head product manager in the sports division of a major online auction company. He has brought you in to help diagnose why his division's profitability is declining and to determine ways to improve the performance.

Key questions to ask:

_____

_____

_____

_____

_____

What are the main issues?

_____

_____

_____

_____

_____

Key approaches/frameworks:

_____

_____

_____

_____

_____

Possible courses of action:

_____

_____

_____

_____

The Practice Range

CASE 6

The CEO of a small to medium-sized sock company has hired your consulting company to assess why profits have been falling from respectable levels 4 years ago to declining 1 year ago to a projected loss this year. You have been assigned to be the main business analyst on the engagement. How would you help analyze the situation and what would be your preliminary recommendations for how to address it?

Key questions to ask:

_____

_____

_____

_____

What are the main issues?

_____

_____

_____

_____

Key approaches/frameworks:

_____

_____

_____

_____

_____

_____

Possible courses of action:

_____

_____

_____

_____

_____

_____

The Practice Range

CASE 7

The COO of a business services company supplying technology consulting to Fortune 500 companies is concerned because she has noticed a downturn in corporate spending overall on consulting and other outsourced services during the trailing two quarters. Upon discussing her thoughts with some of her peers at other tech consulting companies, she has learned that other companies are predicting a reduction in demand for their services as well. She is thinking about how to address this issue within her own company, and has asked for your help in thinking about it as well. What would you like to know, and how would you advise this COO?

Key questions to ask:

_____

_____

What process would you use to investigate this question?

_____

_____

Where would you find the information you need?

_____

_____

CASE 8

Your client is the vice president of global sourcing for a U.S. footwear company. The company once owned seven manufacturing plants in the United States, but now only owns a single plant. The client has brought you in to determine whether to close the final plant. What types of questions would you ask to assist the client in making the right decision?

Key questions to ask:

_____

_____

_____

_____

What are the main issues?

_____

_____

_____

_____

_____

Key approaches/frameworks:

_____

_____

_____

_____

Possible courses of action:

_____

_____

_____

_____

Action recommendations:

_____

_____

_____

_____

Business Strategy Questions

Keep the rules for business strategy questions in mind:

1. Think framework.

2. Ask questions.

3. Work from small to big.

CASE 9

Your client is a large passenger cruise line company. It's considering whether to invest $250 million in a new, 1,500-person passenger ship. The CEO of the company has recently declared publicly that he hopes to deliver 10 percent returns on all major investments. Help the client determine if this is a good investment.

Key questions to ask:

_____

_____

_____

_____

_____

What are the main issues?

_____

_____

_____

_____

_____

Key approaches/frameworks:

_____

_____

_____

_____

Outline for my answer:

_____

_____

_____

_____

Action recommendations:

_____

_____

_____

_____

The Practice Range

CASE 10

Your client is a large regional grocery store player. Most of its stores are located in typical, suburban strip mall–type locations. But that market is almost completely saturated and competition in the grocery industry is fierce, especially with Wal-Mart aggressively expanding its supercenters. The client is looking for new growth options. One idea in front of the CEO is to expand into inner-city communities that have typically been underserved by retailers in general. How might you evaluate this strategic option?

Key questions to ask:

_____

_____

_____

_____

What are the main issues?

_____

_____

_____

_____

Key approaches/frameworks:

Outline for my answer:

Action recommendations:

CASE 11

You have just joined a sportswear clothing company with a long tradition of making polo-style short-sleeve shirts and casual button-down, long-sleeve shirts. Let's call this company Eli's. The division within Eli's that you've joined was formed 6 months before your arrival. This new division designs and manufactures shirts for hip, young, fashion-forward urbanites, made in a similar style to those of several other smaller shirt makers who've burst onto the fashion scene in recent years. Your division is losing a significant amount of money, and your manager has assigned you the project to determine what should be done. What do you need to know, and what would you do to assist your new division at Eli's?

Key questions to ask:

_____

_____

_____

_____

_____

_____

What are the main issues?

_____

_____

_____

Outline for my answer:

_____

_____

_____

Action recommendations:

_____

_____

_____

The Practice Range

CASE 12

Your client is a major sports shoe manufacturer. It has been watching the growth in skateboarding-type shoes in recent years and is wondering whether to start producing these shoes and add them to the existing line. What would you recommend?

Key questions to ask:

_____

_____

_____

What are the main issues?

_____

_____

_____

Outline for my answer:

_____

_____

_____

Resume Questions

Remember the rules for resume questions:

1. Know your story.

2. Keep the Parent Test in mind.

3. Let your excitement shine!

Most people who enter consulting don't make a career out of it. How does consulting fit into your long-range career plans?

CASE 14

I see that last summer you worked for a small printing press. Walk me
through the decision process that led you to work for this company.

I see you used to work in marketing for retail company Z. Did your role and experience there meet your expectations? If so, in what ways was it a good match for your skills? If not, what was the gap and what did you learn from your time in that role?

_____

_____

_____

_____

_____

_____

_____

_____

_____

_____

_____

_____

_____

Nailing the Case

- Market-Sizing Questions

- Business Operations Questions

- Business Strategy Questions

- Resume Questions

The destination is often less important to your interviewer than the road you take to get there.

Now it's time to walk through sample answers to each of the questions posed in "The Practice Range." Although we believe that our recommended answers are good, we know that there are many equally good and even better answers out there. Remember, the destination is often less important to your interviewer than the road you take to get there. With that in mind, smooth sailing! A quick note on the layout: Each question is followed by bad answers (which are admittedly a bit far-fetched in some cases) and a good answer. The questions and dialogue between the hypothetical recruiter and candidate appear in normal type; the WetFeet analysis and commentary appear in italics.

Market-Sizing Questions

Case 1

What is the total number of automobile tires sold in the United States each year?

This is a straightforward market-sizing question, which would be appropriate for undergraduates and advanced-degree candidates.

Bad Answers

- I'd say about one million, give or take.
  The purpose of this kind of case question is not to hear your final answer, but instead to give your interviewer an opportunity to hear how you think about problems with uncertain or unclear information. This answer neither demonstrates the candidate's thinking skills—the set of assumptions and analysis that he did to arrive at his number—nor gives the interviewer anywhere to go in terms of follow-up to assess the candidate's approach to problem solving. In general, never give the answer to a market-sizing question right out of the gate. A better strategy is to take a moment or two to think about what the interviewer is really asking you. In this case, the interviewer is really asking, "Let me see how you would think through developing an estimate for the number of automobile tires sold each year in the United States by telling me about the process and assumptions you'd use to arrive at your estimate."

- Well, it's just four times the number of cars sold in the United States, plus maybe a few more.
  While this offers a small amount of insight into the basic assumptions and thinking that the candidate would use to structure her response, it is not nearly deep or well thought-out enough to satisfy an interviewer—there isn't enough specificity to her answer. While you don't need to arrive at an exact number in your final answer, you do need to provide a decent estimate based on information you either have at hand or can deduce from other information you know.

- All right, this one's easy! My brother is an industry analyst for cars at Goldman and he told me there are 15 million cars sold each year, so my answer is 60 million. Next question.

  Never say that a question you've been asked is easy. If it were easy, it wouldn't be asked of you in a case interview. This answer also implies that the candidate believes one data point or piece of information is all that's required to answer a related—but not perfectly correlated—question. You don't ever want to give the impression that you respond rashly or without measured consideration to a query; this implies immaturity and thoughtlessness, both of which would be very off-putting to an interviewer seeking humble, intelligent, and thoughtful candidates for a role that will often demand maturity and nuanced problem solving.

Good Answer

Candidate: That's an interesting question, considering the various sales channels and the different sources of demand for auto tires in the United States. Let me start by applying a "bottom up" approach towards estimating the total demand for tires.

Good start. The candidate has demonstrated interest in the question and communicated a road map for how he will begin to think out loud about the components of information required to develop a response. Furthermore, the candidate has shown an understanding of both business operations (buzzwords are generally ill advised, but in this case referring to "sales channels" gives the interviewer a sense that the candidate has a basic understanding of operations) and economics (by choosing the demand side of the total market to pursue the market size estimate, rather than the supply side, which is likely to be more challenging in making good assumptions given the relatively arcane nature of tire manufacturing).

Candidate: To begin, I will draw some parameters around the definition of the automobile tires market so that I can then define the sources of demand for tires. In this instance, I'll assume that our market concerns rubber tires for passenger cars and light trucks only. Therefore, I will exclude commercial vehicles, tractors, trailers, and things like RVs for the purposes of my estimate. Is that acceptable, or would you like me to define the market more broadly?

Well done in defining the nature and parameters of the problem before diving in. This demonstrates patience and a desire for precision in defining ambiguous problems before thinking about potential solutions. These are valued skills for consultants and general management strategists, who are hired as much for their maturity in managing complex problems as they are for their ability in solving them. Furthermore, the candidate demonstrates comfort, ease, and most important, respect for his interviewer by asking a question that engages and allows the interviewer to help the candidate define the problem more specifically.

Interviewer: Yes, that's fine. For the purposes of your estimate, just focus on cars and trucks like pickups and SUVs.

Candidate: Okay, sounds good. To start, I believe that one source of demand for automobile tires centers on new cars and trucks themselves. While I don't know offhand what the total number of passenger cars sold each year is, I'll develop a rough estimate that I can use to estimate the tire demand for this channel and then move on. I know that there are about 300 million people in the United States and that about three-quarters of them are above the driving age; this amounts to about 225 million people. I will further assume that about three-quarters of those who are of legal driving age actually own a car; this is based on personal experience with friends and family members in both rural and urban settings. That leaves about 160 million people in the United States who own cars today. Now I'll assume that people replace their cars on average of once every 10 years—just to keep it simple without knowing the exact numbers. That would give an annual estimated number of about 16 million new cars sold, resulting in 64 million new tires sold for those new cars and trucks alone.

The candidate has used a combination of personal knowledge about cars and some round-number estimates using population and demographics to whittle down the new cars element of this market-sizing problem to a manageable and reasonable number. While there may be some inaccurate assumptions in the logic chain the candidate presents here, by speaking his way through the chain with the interviewer, the candidate shows his ability to extrapolate in a reasonable manner using known information to arrive at an estimate when little information was initially available. Using personal experience, like that involving how many friends and family own cars, is okay so long as the candidate doesn't take it too far—which he hasn't. Furthermore, the candidate has driven to a reasonable component of the estimate without taking forever to do so— enough time to think about the logic chain rationally and completely, but not too much time to be burdensome and unnecessary for this estimation exercise.

Candidate: Now that I've estimated the number of tires demanded for new cars and trucks, I'll move on to estimating the number demanded for used cars and trucks currently on the road. I just came up with an estimate of 160 million people who own cars. For the sake of consistency, I'll use this same figure for the estimated number of used cars on the road.

Good job. Realizing that another component of the estimate relies on a piece of information that had previously been estimated, the candidate acknowledges that he has already thought this out and takes a consistent number for the next demand estimate. In doing so, the candidate is being clear on his progress towards an answer and has demonstrated the ability to return to prior thinking to reassess and reuse relevant data when appropriate.

Candidate: Now I need to estimate the average number of years it takes for a driver to wear the tires out on his or her car. I believe I remember from commercials that tires are rated with an average of 60,000- to 80,000-mile warranties. If we assume that an average driver covers about 15,000 miles per year, then that means each car needs its tires replaced in order to stay on the road about once every 4 years. This means about 40 million cars require new tires to replace old worn-out ones each year—approximately 160 million additional new tires for used cars.

The candidate is doing well with one of the rules of market-sizing questions: using nice round numbers that are easy to divide and multiply into other round numbers. This will not only ease and speed up his estimation efforts, but it will also allow him to focus on the assumptions he is making—and communicating those assumptions as he works his way through the answer—rather than on the actual mathematics. You are not being hired for your ability to do cube roots and multiply seven digit numbers in your head. You are being hired to think creatively and logically with uncertain information at hand. Therefore, using round numbers will help you focus on what's important in a market-sizing interview: your thinking, not your math. That said, there is no shame in pulling out a pencil and paper if your case question starts to involve so many numbers or assumptions for a particular estimate that you need to write a few down to keep your thinking straight. Interviewers do not deduct points for candidates who assist their thinking by writing— unless of course all you do is write and you fail to share your progress and thinking at every step with your interviewer. Communication skills are as much a part of the market-sizing interview as are the assumptions and answers you deliver.

Candidate: So, we have what I believe are the two major sources of demand for new auto tires estimated. These add up to 224 million new tires per year.

Interviewer: Have you thought of any other potential sources of demand for new tires? I can think of a few myself. Can you come up with a few more?

The interviewer is trying to put the candidate on the ropes. Her question suggests that the interviewer has a particular answer or idea that she wants the candidate to figure out. Do not get flustered if the interviewer takes this tack at the mid-point in a case interview you believe has been going well. Sometimes it's simply a tactic to assess how a candidate will react under stress. Take a moment, then calmly proceed calmly to develop a more detailed and refined answer. Your interviewer will let you know when you are approaching a sufficient estimate, just as she will let you know that a longer and more detailed estimate is expected.

Candidate: One additional source of demand I haven't addressed yet is flat tires and damaged single tires, both of which need to be replaced on a one-off basis. Would it be helpful to develop an estimate for these tire sales to add to the estimate I've developed so far?

Good job. The candidate demonstrates here that he is able to think about special circumstances, which would add to the market sizing. Although these lesser-order sources of demand or supply in market-sizing questions sometimes do not add materially to the estimated number, it's useful to acknowledge that you consider them and ask the interviewer if she'd like you to augment your estimate with deeper thinking.

Interviewer: That's all right. I believe that you've covered the two largest sources of demand for new auto tires each year, so I think we can settle on 224 million as your estimated annual sales number. I trust you could get a more refined estimate by adding more, smaller sources of new tire demand if we kept pursuing it. We're close enough with what you've given me thus far, so let's move on. Well done.

By simply acknowledging the candidate's ability to go deeper, without actually asking him to do the additional estimating and thinking required, the interviewer demonstrates that she was indeed simply trying to gauge what the candidate's reaction would be to a little pressure or stress in the midst of problem solving. While a little unsettling to a candidate whose confidence may be growing as he moves smoothly through a case, this is by no means out of the ordinary. The candidate did a great job addressing the challenge—and the interviewer acknowledged this by concluding the case in order to use the remaining time in the interview for other problems and discussions. This is a sign that the candidate has done well and has satisfied the interviewer's desire to witness and understand the candidate's logical thinking skills. Well done.

Case 2

What is the average equivalent number of cocoa beans that Hershey's buys each year for its entire U.S. chocolate bar business?

This market-sizing case is one in which it's highly unlikely that you will get anywhere near the actual or real number. In fact, there may not even be a real answer. Instead, the interviewer is purely seeking insight into how you think about large, somewhat undefined problems. In such a case, your best bet is to make a quick decision about whether to drive "bottom up" or "top down" towards an answer and keep working forward as you share your assumptions and math to try to reach a logical end-point.

Bad Answers

- Man, that's a *hard* question! I was expecting some hard questions and I even read up on the companies that you work for, but whoa. . . . That's going to take me forever to figure out. How long are we going to spend on this one? Hold on, I need to get out a pen. . . .
  Freaking out not only has the potential to set off your interviewer, but it's also a waste of time. Calm and tactful reactions to even potentially outlandish questions demonstrate poise. Even if you think a case question is overly hard or obscure, you're better off saying to yourself, "Let me think about how to attack this one," and then collecting your thoughts. Then, start at one end of the problem and begin working through it step by step.

- I don't think that Hershey's actually buys the cocoa beans. I read an article in *Fortune* in which it said that Hershey's buys processed cocoa powder and stores it in a series of ultra-low-humidity casks in its warehouses. In fact, I think I remember the exact tonnage of an average warehouse. Do you want to know it?
  Don't make your interviewer look like an idiot under any circumstances. Even if you know more about a particular topic, demonstrate your thinking rather than your arcane knowledge and you'll make a better impression on the interviewer. As well, arrogance is generally unappealing, but never more so than when it's your only chance to shine in front of someone who has never met you before. Address the question first and foremost.

Good Answer

Candidate: That's going to be quite a large number, given how large a player Hershey's is in the chocolate bar business. That said, I'll need to break this down into parts. Since I don't know too much about the cocoa bean wholesale market, I'll start working towards my answer "top down" by estimating the total market for Hershey's chocolate bars. Once I've got that figured out, I can then multiply by an estimate for the number of cocoa beans it takes to produce the chocolate for one bar.

This is a strong start—and realistically one that would take a moment or two to develop. The candidate has presented a clear layout for how she will attack the problem.

Candidate: I'll start with the annual market for Hershey's chocolate bars. I'm not sure about the number of bars that every supermarket and deli in the United States orders each year. Therefore, I think the best way to come up with an estimate for this is to make an educated guess on how many chocolate bars each person eats in a year and extrapolate for the entire U.S. population.

The candidate is explaining that even though she must make some potentially risky guesses and use them as basic assumptions in order to begin the estimation process, at least she's got a clear structure and line of reasoning to get her to where she needs to go.

Candidate: I know that some of my friends and family members love candy, and on average they will have two or three chocolate bars per week. I myself don't enjoy candy too much and may have one chocolate bar every 2 weeks or so. I know everyone's chocolate taste is a personal thing, but for the sake of simplicity I'll average these out to three chocolate bars every 2 weeks . . . or about six bars per month. Does this seem reasonable?

Although you don't want to pump your interviewer for too much information throughout the case, it's okay to check in on wild leap-of-faith assumptions if you want a little reassurance early on with an assumption that will be the basis for the rest of your estimates.

Interviewer: While that might be a little high, even for someone who loves candy, it's reasonable, so let's assume that's correct for the purposes of this case. Continue . . .

Candidate: Okay. Now, I don't know exactly how much of the market Hershey's possesses for candy bars in the United States, but I know that the company is one of the major industry leaders. Given that M&M/Mars is also a very large chocolate company and that there may be a number of other smaller companies out there, and given that this is a big and very competitive market—which I know based on seeing the myriad candy choices in the checkout aisle each time I shop at the grocery store—I'll assume for simplicity's sake that Hershey's controls one-third of the market. Is there a better percentage I should use here?

Again, checking in on such a key data point is okay. Just don't go overboard with striving for precision in what is fundamentally a case that's full of assumptions and educated guesses. As long as you either communicate your thinking clearly, or check in and ask for data points on key pieces of information about which you have absolutely no idea, you can keep driving towards an answer.

Interviewer: I've never worked on a candy company project either, so I'm not sure. But one-third of the chocolate bar market sounds safe to me as an assumption, so go with it.

The interviewer is readily answering the candidate's questions, indicating that there's no problem with asking them. However, the invitation to keep moving means that the candidate should.

Candidate: Great. So that would mean that an average person in the United States buys two Hershey's chocolate bar products each month—assuming that one-third of their six monthly bars, on average, comprises Hershey's bars— for an annual total of 24 Hershey's chocolate bars. Now I need to multiply this number with the total number of people in the United States.

$$\frac{24}{3} \qquad 7.2\, bil$$

$$\$2.00$$

In a case that's drawn out and potentially confusing, briefly summing up where you are and where you're going—at a logical breaking point—may be a good idea.

Interviewer: Wait. Is it a good assumption that every person in the United States eats an average number of 24 Hershey's chocolate bars?

The interviewer is doing a tactful job of indicating that he wants to lightly challenge one of the assumptions the candidate has made. Don't be alarmed if this happens; it's a natural part of the give and take of an interactive interview. Generally, the correct answer to a question framed like this won't be a "yes" or "no," but rather something like, "Hmmm, let me think about that for a bit."

Candidate: Hmmm, let me think about that for a bit and see if I should revise my assumption.

Good job. The candidate takes the challenge calmly and in style. This is a mature reaction to the natural exchange of potentially conflicting ideas that often occurs in a collaborative business environment—even with colleagues.

Candidate: Now that I've reassessed, I suppose it's likely that the very young and very old portion of the population may not put down so much candy each year. I'm not positive about how age spreads across the U.S. population, but I'll make an aggressive estimate of the number of people in the under-8 and 70- or 75-plus age groups to try to balance out my average candy bar consumption estimate. I'll assume that about 25 percent of the population falls within these ranges, leaving about 75 percent of the population remaining as "active candy eaters."

The candidate maintains her poise, catches on to the gist of the interviewer's question, and delivers a solid answer.

Candidate: So if the United States comprises about 300 million people, 75 percent of that number would equal 225 million. If each of these people eats an average of 24 Hershey's bars every year, that would be . . .

Don't worry about needing to do heavy multiplication—or any other calculator-worthy math—instantly in your head. You don't need to be a savant to be good at business. If numbers get too big, it's okay to think for a moment and just round off to a reasonably close amount or make a few scribbles on a handy sheet of paper to help yourself out. People bring note pads to interviews all the time and barely use them. If the paper's handy and you need it, use it.

Candidate: Let's see . . . that makes 4.5 billion plus 900 million . . . which comes to 5.4 billion Hershey's chocolate bars per year eaten in the United States, according to all of the assumptions I've made so far. Okay, so now I need to estimate the number of cocoa beans that go into each Hershey bar to get the total number of beans. I'm not familiar with the ratio between cocoa beans and chocolate bars, but I do know that lower-grade chocolate is made mostly of sugar and other ingredients and has very little actual pure cocoa. I'll make a quick guess that there are five cocoa beans per bar. So with five beans per bar multiplied with 5.4 billion bars, this yields about 27 billion cocoa beans that Hershey's uses each year for its total U.S. chocolate bar business.

Interviewer: Sounds good. I'll admit I don't know the real answer, but it was interesting to hear how you approached the problem. Good job.

If the final number you arrive at doesn't pass your sanity test because it just seems to be way too high or too low, then don't hesitate to take a moment and think through all of the key assumptions that served as the basis for your final answer. If it does makes sense and passes your final gut check, then you're good to go.

Case 3

How many pages of paper would it take to completely encircle the earth at the equator?

This is a reasonably straightforward market-sizing question that is perhaps deceptively simple—be forewarned that some wrinkles may emerge. This question would be appropriate for undergrads and advanced-degree candidates.

Bad Answers

- That's a stupid question. Why are these case interviews always so random? I'm trying to get a consulting job. I didn't go to a top school to do silly estimates about the size of the earth.
  It's never a smart move to insult the interviewer or the process. The case interview process is what it is and you're not going to change it. Plus, although no system is perfect, it has actually proven to be a fairly good predictor of consulting success. In fact, if you don't enjoy the mental gymnastics of doing these problems, you probably won't enjoy consulting.

- I have no idea. I don't know anything about the size of the earth. I was an English major. I thought these would be business cases.
  While not as bad as opening by insulting the process, giving up or "punting" is clearly not the way to go either. You almost certainly will get a question whose topic is unfamiliar to you. That's part of the game. Buck up, use any related knowledge you do have, create a structure, and start making some clear assumptions.

Good Answer

Candidate: Well, that's certainly an interesting question. I must admit, I don't know much at all about the size of the earth. Nevertheless, I'll give it my best shot and try to use what I do know, and I'll talk you through my thinking.

Good start. The candidate admits to a hole in his knowledge, so the interviewer might be willing to cut him some slack initially. But the candidate also indicates his willingness to attack the problem and bring to bear what he does know. This is an important trait that interviewers are looking for. Plus, the candidate is most likely a bit nervous since he's not comfortable with the topic. A bit of initial reflection (remember to speak slowly and clearly) can calm you down as well as give you time to think!

Candidate: Well, let's start with the paper, since I do know a thing or two about that. You know, it strikes me that the easiest way to tackle the situation would be to consider the paper lengthwise. It's common knowledge that a standard sheet of paper is 8.5 inches by 11 inches. Since 11 inches is pretty close to one foot, I'll just consider a sheet of paper to be 1 foot long.

Interviewer: That's pretty clever. I must admit that I was originally thinking you'd consider the thickness of the sheet of paper, since that's obviously more complicated. But I like your style. You made a solid assumption and chose a path of less resistance. However, I reserve the right to ask you for a different version later in the interview.

Score one for the candidate. He's made a great assumption. Remember: round numbers, straightforward assumptions. Don't make things harder than they have to be.

Candidate: Okay, now for the hard part: the stuff I don't know as well. Let's see. I'll start with something I do know. I've taken a bunch of trips from New York to Los Angeles, and I'm pretty sure that the distance between them is roughly 3,000 miles. I'm going to assume this is right if that's okay with you.

Solid start. Anchor in something you know and go from there. Your interviewer will tell you if she has a problem with your assumption. Otherwise, forge ahead.

Candidate: I'd say there are a few ways to come at this. If I know that the USA is about 3,000 miles across and I then picture the handful of globes I've seen in libraries and such, it seems to me that you could fit about ten USA's around the center of the earth. That would imply 30,000 miles. I'll just assume a mile is around 5,000 feet and therefore that implies 150,000,000 feet. Given my 1-foot assumption for the length of the paper, this equates to 150,000,000 sheets of paper. I know there's some rounding there, but I've at least rounded up on the paper size and down on the mile size.

Excellent round one. Nice round numbers, solid assumptions, awareness of the assumptions, and a decent first answer. This would almost be good enough, but the candidate is a star, so he isn't done.

Candidate: But I want to double check this estimation if that's okay? The 30,000-mile figure feels about right, but let's look at it another way. I'm pretty comfortable with the 3,000 miles being the distance spanning the USA. And I know that it takes about 5 hours to fly from New York to Los Angeles. That feels about right, because I seem to recall reading that 747s fly at about 600 miles per hour. So let me use those numbers to gut check my figures. I think it's about 8 hours from Los Angeles to Tokyo, so let's call that 5,000 miles. So now I'm at 8,000 miles from New York to Tokyo.

This is a good approach: The candidate is using what he knows. When you've got a lot of data floating around, you've really got to make an effort to keep it all straight. Don't be afraid to write things down.

Next I'll go from Tokyo across Russia. I have no idea what that flying time is, but I know it's long. I know Russia is huge: the world's biggest country. I think it has something like ten time zones. So I bet it's about three times bigger than the USA. Therefore, I'm going to say its 9,000 miles across. Now I'm at 17,000 miles from New York to the Ural Mountains. I've never flown across Europe, but folks are always saying the European Union is similar in size and population to the USA, so why don't I say it's the same 3,000 miles across? I think that's high, but it's close enough. That puts me at 20,000 miles so far. I've flown from London to New York and it takes about 5 hours. So, let's say that distance is 3,000 miles, the same as it is for New York to Los Angeles. That puts me at 23,000 miles total. Of course, I've been flying up in the northern hemisphere for the most part—the distance is greater at the equator. I'll tack on another couple thousand miles and call it an even 25,000. That's within shouting distance of my original 30,000, so I'm feeling more comfortable. In this case,

I'd multiply 25,000 by 5,000 to get 125,000,000 pages of paper. Therefore, if I wanted to take a final step, I could average the two estimates and come out with somewhere between 130,000,000 and 140,000,000 sheets of paper.

Interviewer: That's pretty impressive for someone who didn't know anything about the size of the earth. Just be glad I didn't ask you about the distance to the sun (it's 93 million miles, by the way). I warned you at the beginning, though, that I might ask for a different version, so now you'll have to humor me: Let's quickly suppose you have to consider the thickness of the paper, not the length or the width.

Candidate: Okay, that should be straightforward enough. Paper's pretty thin—too thin for me to think about it in terms of individual pieces. But I do have some experience loading laser printers (don't we all!). I know one of those packs of paper has 500 sheets, and I'd say it's about 3 inches thick. So that tells me there are 2,000 sheets of paper in a foot if you consider the thickness of the paper. Therefore, if we take my rough 130,000,000 feet estimate and multiply that by 2,000, we get 260,000,000,000 sheets of paper at the equator. Let me check my zeros. . . . Yep, that's my estimate.

Well done! The candidate has demonstrated a facility with numbers, a stick-to-it-ive-ness, enthusiasm, creativity, and an ability to apply past learning to current problems. The candidate has responded to interviewer prompts and come up with reasonable answers that he's tested. It's certainly likely that somebody with no idea of the circumference of the earth would also have very little knowledge of the distances from various cities. No matter. The point is that there are many ways to skin a cat. One quick point: Even in round number examples like this one, it's easy to get lost in the commas and zeros. Don't be afraid to use pen and paper to keep things straight.

Case 4

How many pay phones are there in Manhattan?

This is a fairly straightforward market-sizing question, which would be appropriate for undergraduates and advanced-degree candidates.

Bad Answers

- No one uses phone booths anymore. Everyone has a cell. There are hardly any booths anymore, except for the one in that Colin Farrell movie.
  Not a smart angle. Despite showing a knowledge of pop culture, your interviewer will not be amused.

- I saw that annoying Verizon guy in the *New York Times* yesterday. The article he was in stated that there are 6,360 payphones in Manhattan. I have a photographic memory, so there's your answer.
  Even if you know the answer, the more important thing is still the process. You may want to admit that you know the answer in case the interviewer wants to change the question. Either way, you still need to give a solid case interview answer to this question.

- How am I supposed to know anything about Manhattan? I've never been there. I'm from Paris/San Francisco/Des Moines . . .
  This might be a fair point. It's tough when you get a question that pertains to a topic about which you know nothing. And to be fair, if your interviewer knows that you have absolutely no experience with Manhattan, he likely won't ask you this question. But then again, maybe he will. So be ready. If you are indeed from Paris, jump in and say something like, "Well, I'm sorry, I know next to nothing about Manhattan. But I know it's a big city and I come from Paris, another big city. So I'll just use what I know about Paris and try to extrapolate from there. . . ." Your interviewer should be fine with this tactic. If he's not, he'll probably provide some additional information to help get you started.

Good Answer

Candidate: There are a couple of ways to go about answering this question, so I'll try to break it down into parts. I figure I'm going to have to come up with some notion of the size of Manhattan and also the likely locations of pay phones. I'll start with the size of Manhattan.

Good start. The candidate has successfully laid out two key pieces of data needed and has created a logical structure to use in walking the interviewer towards the answer.

Candidate: While I don't know Manhattan intimately, I do know there's a grid system in much of the city, which should help us immeasurably. I know it doesn't cover the entire city and I know there are some non-numbered avenues in there like Park and Broadway, but I'll try to make some round assumptions. I know the streets go at least as high as 125th Street in Harlem. And I think they go even higher, at least to 175th Street if I correctly recall the time I drove down into Manhattan. Plus, I know the southern tip of the island, the older part, doesn't have the grid. For example, down by Wall Street, it's kind of haphazard, like downtown Boston. So when I put all that together, I'm going to say there are 200 streets running east to west in Manhattan. In terms of those running north to south, I know that there are somewhat more than ten avenues, plus the named, non-numbered streets. I will therefore say there are 15 streets running north to south. That leaves me with 200 **x** 15 = 3,000 intersections. I'm going to think in terms of intersections and blocks, since I think that's easiest. Here, I've been scratching this down in a rough map; this is how I'm looking at it. I know there are some exceptions to the rules I've laid out, but my assumptions seem solid and the variations will likely balance each other out. Does this seem okay with you?

Good job. The candidate is developing the structure and has quickly pulled together a number of solid assumptions. There were other bases for these assumptions, including land area or population, but the grid appears to be the easiest way to come up with them. The candidate has done well in making round-number assumptions. The interviewer is fine with his approach, so the candidate should keep on moving.

Candidate: Now let me think about locations of pay phones. I suppose to keep it simple we can think about pay phones that are outside and pay phones that are inside. Outside areas will include things like street corners and the sides of buildings. Inside would be lobbies of buildings and such. I think there will be very few pay phones in residential buildings, so we are mostly talking office buildings, restaurants, and hotels.

Another good, quick summary that still has the candidate moving ahead confidently.

Candidate: I'll start with the outdoor phones. I know I have the aforementioned 3,000 intersections. And there are four corners to every intersection. Now, I know some corners have no phones and others have a bank of phones. And that's not even covering the banks of phones that sometimes appear mid-block on the sides of buildings. There are a lot of angles to consider, so I'll make the assumption that every other corner of every intersection has one phone, meaning two per intersection, meaning 6,000 outside phones in Manhattan. This number seems a little high to me, so why don't I make it 5,000.

This is a good piece of thinking. Clear, methodical assumptions with solid math. Stating your gut feel is okay, too. Those reactions can be valuable and often right. In a real-world situation, a gut feel might cause you to re-evaluate a position or try another angle. But for now, the interviewer is satisfied and so the candidate can move on.

Next, I have to come up with the number of pay phones inside buildings. This could potentially be pretty complicated, what with restaurants, office buildings, hotels, and so on. Would you like me to be very granular here or shall I make some broader assumptions?

This is a reasonable question. The candidate is not trying to get off easy, but rather stating the facts. If there's enough time, the interviewer may allow the candidate to slog through a bunch of specific assumptions about types of establishments. In this case, she tells the candidate to make some broader assumptions.

Candidate: Okay, I'll try to keep it broad. If I think about an intersection, there's probably an average of one restaurant, one office building, and a quarter of a hotel. This is assuming that on average each block is mostly residential. Let's just say there is one pay phone in the lobby of each type of building. I realize that some will have many more, but some might have none. So if I use my 3,000 intersections, that means 3,000 x 2.25. . . . Well, that's going to be more than 6,000, which added to the 5,000 equates to 11,000 pay phones. That number seems too high. I'm going to revise my estimate and say there's one inside pay phone per intersection, which means 3,000 inside pay phones, which means 8,000 total. Hmmm. That still feels a bit high to me, but the assumptions seemed reasonable along the way. What do you think? Should I start over?

Interviewer: That's fine. I actually don't know the exact answer anyway. What I wanted was your thought process and it's been good so far. Let's look at your little map sketch, though, and think through briefly what wrinkles or other assumptions you'd test if you had more time. Just run through them for me.

In some cases, your interviewer will not know the exact answer. Once again, that's because the exact answer doesn't matter. The process does, however, along with your performance and attitude. In this case, the candidate's gut reaction was effective and relevant and has led to this final chance to shine.

Candidate: There are a number of things I'd look at. First of all, you've got Central Park sitting in the middle of Manhattan. And it's big. So that would be a big hole in my grid assumptions. You'd have to knock out a lot of intersections. Next, you have the issue of the streets and the avenues on the edge of the island only having one or two accessible corners, not always four. Finally, when looking at the number of buildings in a block, I'd probably be better off thinking in square blocks, since buildings are large. Finally, because my gut tells me the results aren't quite right, I'd want to triangulate with some more methods. Probably a course of assumptions using phones per population would be reasonable.

A fine effort. This question was deceptively simple, but the candidate has done a good job. The lesson as always: You don't have to be right, but you do have to do the case right. Make good assumptions, nail the math, listen to your gut reactions, summarize, talk out loud, lay out a plan, and follow it. All these things are what count. This is a case in which jotting down thoughts or the map in this case will help you a great deal.

Business Operations Questions

Case 5

Your client is the head product manager in the sports division of a major online auction company. He has brought you in to help diagnose why his division's profitability is declining and to determine ways to improve the performance.

This is a very open-ended, but fairly straightforward, operations question. It will require the candidate to quickly assess the root causes of the problem and to identify solutions. For these types of questions, no preordained framework is required (although you will see that the candidate does throw a clever one in halfway through the case). For the most part, the interviewer is simply looking for a structured answer.

Bad Answer

I don't participate a lot in online auctions, so I don't know a lot about how they work. Can you ask me another question?

The interviewer is not asking for domain-relevant expertise. As a general rule, if you don't know, just ask.

Good Answer

Candidate: Okay. So there are two questions you're asking: (1) Why is profitability declining; and (2) How can we improve performance? Let's focus on the first question, because then I'll feel better equipped to answer the second.

The candidate has stated the obvious, but has given the interviewer a very simple road map for where he's going to go with the case.

Candidate: There are two possible answers to the first question: either revenues are going down relative to costs, or costs are going up relative to revenues. Because I'm not that familiar with online auction sites, and don't want to make any unrealistic assumptions in my diagnosis, can you tell me generally how the client's business model works?

The candidate realizes that it will serve him better to ask questions up front than to make faulty assumptions.

Interviewer: At the risk of oversimplifying, the client's online auction model is structured as follows: Sellers pay a fixed fee—50 cents—to the client to list their products. If their products are purchased, the sellers pay an additional fee, equal to a fixed percentage (5 percent) of the sale price of that item. So, for example, if the seller is listing a bowling ball that sells for $100, the client's revenue would be $5.50.

Candidate: So all of the revenue comes from the sellers. This is a free service to the buyers.

Interviewer: That's correct.

Candidate: And are there any other revenue streams?

Interviewer: Not at this point.

Candidate: So what about the cost side of the equation? How does that work?

Interviewer: Good question, and I'm going to try to help you answer that one. There's only one platform for the entire auction site. What do you think this means for the client?

The interviewer has answered enough questions and is ready for the candidate to stop using the Socratic method.

Candidate: If these platform-related costs—hardware and software, I would imagine—are centralized, this probably means that the client has little control over some of the costs of his business, for example site development and online merchandising. Does he have any dedicated costs to his business, for example people or a marketing budget?

Interviewer: The client has 12 people reporting to him and a small marketing budget.

Candidate: Have any of these direct costs changed significantly over time?

Interviewer: No.

Candidate: Okay. I'm going to make the assumption that these centralized costs are not the reason for the lagging profitability. Plus, it sounds like our client wouldn't have a lot of control over them even if they were. So let's ignore those for now. In addition, because the other costs have not changed significantly over time, I feel confident in concluding that the problem with the client's business is on the revenue side. Let's talk about what's going on there.

The candidate has made some broad assumptions, but they are grounded in reality. He has also showed an ability to use those assumptions to make a reasonable conclusion.

Candidate: There are two hypotheses that quickly come to mind. One is that there aren't enough buyers on the site—that is to say, there are a lot of sports items up for auction, but there aren't a lot of people bidding on them. The other is that the client is facing a supply problem, meaning there isn't enough merchandise up on the site to sustain the business. Let me test these two hypotheses in turn.

Again, a very simple road map for where the candidate is going to take the case. If the candidate is way off here (which he is not), the interviewer would be able to stop the candidate and steer him in the right direction.

Interviewer: Sounds like a decent structure to me. What are the types of analyses you would do to determine whether your hypotheses are true or not?

Proposing the right analyses to support or deny an assumption is one of the most critical skills in consulting. The interviewer is testing the candidate and will be looking for very specific analyses.

Candidate: I would do several analyses to determine whether there were enough buyers on the site. One would simply be to assess the total number of visits to the overall auction site over time. This would give me a sense of how popular the site is.

Interviewer: And how would you assess the results?

Candidate: One would hope that the number of visits to the site is increasing— or at least staying constant.

Interviewer: But if there are a lot of people visiting the site, but no one is purchasing anything, then those hits aren't very valuable, are they?

The interviewer is challenging the candidate's thinking, pushing him to be thoughtful in his analyses. The interviewer is also gauging how the candidate will react to this "bad cop" attitude.

Candidate: Good point. Let me revise my proposal: I would want to look not only at overall visits to the site, but also the number of products purchased.

Interviewer: Right. This is what's called the conversion rate. So let's say that overall hits and purchases have been increasing steadily, but in the sports category the conversion rate has dropped significantly over the past year. And the client is feeling pressure because his business is dragging down the otherwise stellar performance of the rest of the organization.

More useful information. Make sure that when the interviewer offers you data, you use it.

Candidate: What this says to me is that the attractiveness of the overall product offering has declined: On a relative basis, the number of purchases has lagged the number of visits, thus decreasing the conversion rate. Can you tell me whether the product mix or marketing has changed, or whether the site navigation—how you get to the site—has changed?

Note here how the candidate has used a simple marketing framework—the 4P framework—and adapted it to the case without making it blatant. He didn't introduce the framework as such, and substituted words such as "site navigation" for "placement" and "marketing" for "promotion." Also, since the interviewer already told the candidate that one of the P's—price—was standard across the entire site, and therefore not under the control of the client, the candidate astutely left it out of his response.

Interviewer: All good questions. In fact, only the product mix has really changed. Both marketing and site navigation have remained constant. The product mix, which at one point was more focused on outdoor recreational sporting activities—for example tents, water skis, and so on—has shifted more to sports clothing.

Candidate: Is there any data to explain why this took place?

Interviewer: Let me turn the question back to you. How might you get this data?

Candidate: Both buyers and sellers, I'm assuming, need to provide e-mail addresses. The client could do a survey, offering rewards in return for filling out a survey on why certain items did or did not sell.

Interviewer: Good idea. What type of rewards might these be?

The candidate is wandering a little off of his framework, but the interviewer is allowing him to do so. Because the candidate offered such a solid road map for where he was going with his 4P framework, he can easily move back on to his original path when the interviewer prompts him to do so.

Candidate: For the seller, this might be a series of free listings. For the buyer, it might be a certain credit to his or her account for the next purchase.

Interviewer: And this is exactly what happened. What the client found was that the value equation for outdoor equipment did not work online. Though the prices were good on the site—for example, a high-quality frame backpack for $75—the shipping costs (borne by the buyer) made it too costly for the buyer, and the packing requirements to ship the good were too onerous for the seller.

Candidate: I see. So what likely happened is that the model quickly broke down: The buyers left because they didn't see the value, and the sellers left because there were no buyers. So, to answer my two hypotheses around whether this was a supply problem or a demand problem, the answer is yes to both because they are absolutely linked. Fewer buyers leads to fewer sellers, which leads to fewer buyers and so on.

The candidate has scored big points by answering his initial hypotheses and understanding that they are not mutually exclusive. If he had introduced the phrase "virtuous circle" here, he may have been offered the job on the spot—consultants live for the virtuous circle.

Candidate: So it probably follows that if the marketing programs are the same, the client is targeting the wrong consumer segment; instead of going after recreational sports buyers and sellers, the client should switch its focus to buyers who want sports clothing.

Interviewer: And how would you go about targeting this audience?

Candidate: I would want to know who the consumer is—what the demographics are, how and where the consumer is currently shopping, what types of clothing are most popular. And then I would want to locate sellers. The Internet is probably a new and potentially interesting channel for mom-and-pop stores that sell sports clothing. Perhaps signing up more of these sellers could entice more buyers to come—and buy—on the sports site.

The candidate has suggested some simple and basic ideas for how the client could proceed. More important, he has used a structured and straightforward way to answer the case question, and has gotten to the heart of the business problem—the infamous virtuous circle. Well done!

Case 6

The CEO of a small- to medium-sized sock company has hired your consulting company to assess why profits have been falling from respectable levels 4 years ago to declining 1 year ago to a projected loss this year. You have been assigned to be the main business analyst on the engagement. How would you help analyze the situation and what would be your preliminary recommendations for how to address it?

You will notice that this is a question about profitability that is similar to the last operations case, but the candidate (who gives the "good answer") takes a very different approach.

Bad Answer

Candidate: I'd basically just find out what the problem is by talking to all of the employees and doing a bunch of market research, and then I'd talk about it with my consulting team and figure out what the best thing would be to do.

Wow, that's really specific. Thanks for the high-level tutorial on how consulting works. Whenever possible, avoid extremely general answers. Although a standard approach to assessing problems and evaluating potential solutions is helpful, don't stay up in the clouds—you need to focus on the business problem at hand.

Interviewer: Yes, that's generally what consultants do. But what would you specifically want to focus on in this case?

The interviewer was tactful in delivering the message, "Get on with it. Let me see how you think."

Candidate: Well, it seems to me that sandals, clogs, and Tevas are getting more popular all the time. I'd guess that the market for socks is shrinking these days since not as many people are wearing formal shoes; it must be that the market is just drying up. I'd recommend that the company look at other products it can produce that are more popular.

With this assessment and recommendation, the candidate will be in sandals often since he will be sitting at home—rather than in an office—looking through the want ads. Guessing at the heart of the problem without gathering any background information is always a bad idea; it's the equivalent of shooting at a target in a dark room. You might hit the target, but it's more likely that you won't. Even if you do, it won't be a successful interview anyway. The interviewer wants to see how well you ask for help in finding the light switch, what you'd look for in the room once the lights are on in order to find your target, and how you'd aim before you fire at it (to take the analogy to its conclusion). In practical terms, profits may or may not be related to market expansion or contraction. And there are many ways—not just one—to deal with a shrinking market and still be profitable. More information is needed, and the candidate should have tempered the urge to skip ahead to a recommendation before investigating the situation.

Good Answer

Candidate: If profits are down, then either the sock company's costs are up, revenues are down, or both. I'd first want to understand the cost side of the equation at a high level to see whether there are any red flags on the operating side of things. Have costs increased for this company in recent years?

The candidate has successfully recognized this as a profit question. Furthermore, the candidate has chosen one of the key issues in profitability to investigate first: costs and operating efficiency.

Interviewer: Actually, no. I can tell you that costs have even declined a bit as a proportion of revenues as the client has improved sourcing in its materials and has automated one of its weaving plants. Margins were looking pretty good after the plant investment until a couple of years ago, when things took a turn for the worse.

So it's not costs. Carry on with information gathering. The interviewer, role-playing as the client, has actually given a hint in the bit of extra information he shared after answering the candidate's core question.

Candidate: Okay, so if the problem is not fundamentally on the cost side, it must be on the revenue side. Since revenues are a function of product sales volume and the average price of its products, I'd want to understand a little more about what's going on with each one to dig further on where the problem may lie. Has the overall market for socks of the sort that this company produces been shrinking in the last few years?

The candidate has wisely decided to start by understanding the current dynamics of the industry. Doing so will allow her to determine whether she's dealing with a market share or a market-size problem. Furthermore, the candidate has identified price and volume as the component parts of revenue and has done a good job explicitly communicating this knowledge to the interviewer by saying it out loud. The candidate asked the question to understand if there are macro issues affecting the client's business—a contraction in demand for the client's products that is outside of the client's control.

Interviewer: The market is in relatively good shape, actually. Overall demand for socks like the ones the company produces has been steadily increasing in line with population growth. So, the problem isn't with the demand for these products.

The candidate is now getting close to the heart of the matter. Since it's not a market-size issue, then it must be a market-share issue.

Candidate: All right. What's happening with the company's sales volume and pricing, then? If the market is healthy but the client's profits are declining even though costs are in good shape, I would assume that the client is experiencing a rapid decline in sales. How have sales volume and average prices been doing for the past couple of years?

The candidate is starting to test a theory—that a decline in sales is hurting profitability. This is a common source of profit loss in industries with high fixed production costs; basically, operating costs cannot be reduced as quickly as falling revenues to protect margins due to big fixed expenses like plants and warehouses, which have lower costs-per-unit as production volumes go up but higher costs-per-unit when production volumes fall. By not only asking about sales volumes, but also about pricing, the candidate is probing to find out if unit sales are falling as well as the potential reason why: competition (which often hurts not only sales volumes but also prices for former market leaders who experience price pressure and often must lower prices to remain competitive).

Interviewer: That's really two questions in one, but they are both relevant here. Yes, sales volumes are falling precipitously. And prices for this client's products have been falling too.

The candidate continues to make good progress through her framework and has identified the forces at work in creating the profit problem. Now she has enough to make a prediction about what's going on and formulate a few potential recommendations.

Candidate: Right. So not only is the client seeing lower revenues, which is probably hurting profitability if that automated plant is suddenly more costly on a per-unit basis than it was before volumes fell, but also the profit margin is getting squeezed by lower average price per unit sold. Given what I know now, I'm going to guess that a growing market for these kinds of socks has attracted a number of new competitors in recent years. I'd guess that these new competitors are stealing market share from the client with similar or better products, and by consequence the client is dropping prices in an effort to retain the share they are losing and boost sales volumes. Does that sound about right?

Interviewer: That's a pretty good guess. Your theory that falling sales and prices are due to the entry of numerous new competitors is correct. So what do you think the client should do about it?

This part of the case is where there is a transition from the analytical to the practical—time to step out of the land of theory and into the land of reality. If the candidate doesn't have a great deal of practical business experience to guide her thinking in how to address the problem once it's identified, that's not a show-stopper. The interviewer will already know that this is the case by having reviewed the candidate's resume. As such, he will likely cut her a little slack so long as the recommendations are framed as possibilities rather than conclusive solutions. Remember: If you have less confidence in your recommendation in a case interview, then consider several possible approaches to dealing with the problem and share them all in turn. This will show that you keep an open mind with challenging problems and don't settle on one solution too quickly—a valuable skill in the kind of team-oriented business practice that is common among leading companies and consulting firms alike.

Candidate: Well, I believe there are several different potential paths for the client to take to address the impact that competition is having on profits. Therefore, I'd want to make several different possible recommendations and then review each recommendation's potential with my colleagues—they are likely to have more experience dealing with this type of situation.

Good job. This could be perceived as stalling, but in fact it shows a balanced and collaborative approach on the part of the candidate.

Interviewer: I can see why you'd want to do that. It always makes sense to review ideas with colleagues before rushing in to give the client one answer only. That said, I'm interested in hearing a few of your ideas. What are a couple potential ideas you'd present to your team to consider as recommendations for the client in this case?

Though the interviewer values the candidate's response, he is not going to let her off the hook and close the case out before hearing at least a few of the candidate's specific ideas. No problem. Do a quick priority of what you consider to be the best ideas in your arsenal and share the top two to keep things moving forward.

Candidate: Well, one idea would be for the client to address the competitive threat head-on by assessing the qualities and value proposition of the products that are stealing market share. In this way, the client can learn if making improvements to the product will make it more competitive, thus earning back some of the lost share—and possibly justifying a higher price in the process.

Good. The candidate has proposed a logical potential solution to address the key source of the profitability problem: market share loss.

Interviewer: Hmmm, that's one interesting idea and it seems to make sense. But what if the client's product development time is too long for this to be viable? Or what if the client lacks the time, resources, and money to really investigate and respond to what's driving competitors' products to take away share?

The interviewer hasn't entirely discounted this potential solution, but he is trying to push the candidate to consider limitations on the client side that could reduce the viability of this recommendation. He wants the candidate to consider an even more real-world perspective— taking into account both how the market and the client's organization might react to a recommendation. The candidate should continue further and present her second recommendation and see if that one is perhaps more viable.

Candidate: If that's the case, I have another potential recommendation. If the client cannot assess and change its product offerings fast enough to combat the competitive threat in the marketplace, then the client might want to consider making a quick acquisition of one of its competitors in order to regain some share. If the client has enough cash on the books to make this viable, it could be a way to "buy" rather than "make" new products that better compete in the market and thereby increase profits.

The candidate has risen to the interviewer's challenge by calling on the classic "make vs. buy" strategy when evaluating a response to competitive threats. Would you be expected to come up with two such strong recommendations, both well grounded in practical business? Not necessarily. It's clear that this candidate is obviously experienced enough to quickly formulate a short list of solid suggestions. When asked for potential practical solutions to a problem, be fact-based, rely on what you've learned in the case so far, and be creative but not outlandish.

Interviewer: Yes, that's another potential way to go for this client, and you're right that this may be more practical if the product development and launch times are long. There are undoubtedly other potential recommendations you could make, but for now that's sufficient for me to see your line of reasoning on how you'd address the core issue. Good job. Let's move on.

Well done. The candidate gets bonus points from the interviewer for understanding the "make vs. buy" decision that many companies face when under intense competitive pressure. Having done admirably on this case, the candidate should feel good about moving forward with the interview.

Case 7

The COO of a business services company supplying technology consulting to Fortune 500 companies is concerned because she has noticed a downturn in corporate spending overall on consulting and other outsourced services during the trailing two quarters. Upon discussing her thoughts with some of her peers at other tech consulting companies, she has learned that other companies are predicting a reduction in demand for their services as well. She is thinking about how to address this issue within her own company, and has asked for your help in thinking about it as well. What would you like to know, and how would you advise this COO?

Many business operations cases set up the situation you need to consider in this way: The candidate is asked to consider how changes in the marketplace will impact a company and what some of the operational responses could be to these changes. This case is indicative of the changing nature of business in the United States in that it focuses on a professional services company—not a traditional manufacturing or other packaged goods company. This means that the operational issues—and costs—the candidate will want to consider are different from those relevant to a manufacturing company.

Bad Answers

- I'm surprised she was able to talk to other companies. I thought that all of the consulting firms were really secretive and didn't share information because of client confidentiality rules and whatnot. My brother is a consultant, and he can't even tell me what clients he's working for—just the general terms like "telecommunications company" and that kind of thing. So maybe the COO is getting bad information or getting lied to—she should think about doing some research to see if her peers are giving her the straight scoop on what's happening with their businesses.

  It's a waste of everyone's time to question the very information presented in the case itself. In general, whatever you are told by the interviewer towards setting up the case, you should trust. Focus on moving things forward throughout the case, rather than right off the bat questioning the very foundation of the case itself.

- I think she should start firing people and find a start-up to sublease some of her real estate. Sounds like the boom times are over, so she's going to need to cut the fat.

The candidate is moving much too quickly towards a recommendation. He hasn't investigated the issues at all. Until it's clear what the operational dynamics and concerns are for the COO in this case, the candidate should avoid jumping to potentially callous or impractical conclusions.

Good Answer

Candidate: This is an interesting case since it involves a services company, rather than a manufacturing company; this means the COO is going to be managing a different set of operations costs and processes as compared to those of manufacturing or other companies of that ilk. Since you've told me that marketplace demand is contracting for her and other companies' services, I'm going to assume that this is not going to change for some time and that the COO's main challenge is going to be cost containment as her revenues stagnate or fall in the short term.

This is a strong start. The candidate has inferred key information from the set-up of the case—namely that overall industry demand is contracting and that this is likely to negatively impact revenues. The candidate has further communicated that he understands the profit equation—and that costs, rather than revenues, are the relevant variable for the COO to focus on since revenues are assumed to be falling due to forces outside of the COO's control.

Interviewer: That's a safe assumption. When the overall industry is experiencing a downturn, it's important to focus on the cost side of the equation to defend profitability. What do you think is important to consider in this regard?

The interviewer is validating that cost management is at the heart of the matter. The candidate should move forward with an analysis of the operational costs that a company like this one would be working hardest at managing—in other words, he should work towards figuring out which operational costs are the most significant or require the most attention.

Candidate: In a general sense, I would want to think about how to manage operational expenses, which break down into fixed costs and variable costs. From what I know about consulting companies like this one, the main fixed costs tend to be things related to keeping the company running—like technology resources, real estate costs for the headquarters and branch offices, and administrative support for core functions like human resources, finance, and facilities.

The candidate is continuing to show good knowledge of both the theory of operating costs and the practical application to a services business—by listing the specific components of the typical fixed costs for a company like this one. Of course, a focus on fixed costs for a manufacturing company would include many of these items as well as key additional fixed costs like plants, machinery, and other fixed assets related to the production of goods.

Interviewer: Yes, that's correct. Those are the main fixed costs that the COO manages for her company. Are there other costs she should think about?

Candidate: Yes, the client would also need to think about the variable costs she manages. In this case, I believe that the main variable costs are the salaries of the professional services staff that the company employs to actually do the billable work of technology consulting. It may be a bit harsh to call these people "variable costs," but it's my understanding that most companies think of their labor force as one of the variable resources that the management team must handle in terms of cost.

Interviewer: Yes, employee salaries are a big component of the variable costs that the COO needs to consider. Are there any others?

The candidate has correctly identified employee salaries as one of the main variable operating costs. However, he should try to take a comprehensive view of the landscape by identifying one or two other variable costs that might impact the cost side of the profitability equation.

Candidate: Yes, some other variable costs that the COO is managing would include travel and expenses related to her staff's client service work, compensation for contractors and other part-time workers, supplies and other nonfixed assets used to run the business, and selling and R&D expenses related to finding new clients and developing new service offerings.

Interviewer: Good job. That's a pretty solid list of the fixed and variable costs that the COO would want to consider in thinking about how to address the company's profitability with revenues declining. So what would you suggest she do to improve things?

The interviewer is getting into the heart of the matter now—he has acknowledged that the candidate has done a solid job in applying business theory to the case by communicating the profit equation, breaking down costs into fixed and variable, and listing the specific costs that fall under each category. The interviewer now wants to go deeper and really see what the candidate's practical business experience and instincts lead him to recommend.

Candidate: Well, let's consider each of the cost categories in turn. In regard to fixed costs, most of the ones I mentioned are very difficult to reduce or impact on a short-term basis. It's the very fact that they are hard to change that makes us think of them as fixed in the near term. If the COO needed to make drastic changes, perhaps she could consider reducing the real estate budget by tightening down the floor plans and using less real estate space for existing resources. While this may not be a popular decision, it might be possible to reduce the monthly real estate lease fees—or gain some subleasing rents if the company owns its headquarters buildings and can free enough space to take on new tenants. This is a challenging prospect though, if we assume that the company is managing its space fairly efficiently already. I believe it would be more fruitful to focus on reducing or containing variable costs instead.

Sometimes you've got to go with your instincts and make a judgment call about where to focus your thinking and recommendations. This is fine to do—the interview time is limited after all.

Interviewer: I can see why you'd want to do that. These are the costs that the COO is most likely to be able to impact in the short run. So what do you suggest she consider doing?

Candidate: In tight times, I know that one of the things that gets cut first is budgets for new resources like technology expenditures, office supplies, company perquisites, incentive trips, and so on. One suggestion would be to have the COO ask her department managers to revisit their operating cost budgets and identify areas where they can reduce nonvital expenditures for the next several quarters in an effort to help boost profitability. Investing in internal resources tends to stall or get scaled back when times are tough, and as long as she communicates why this needs to happen, then her division managers should understand and be able to deliver some cost savings. Marketing and branding budgets could also be reduced if her company is spending significant money in these areas. After all, these budgets go towards increasing market share— something that may not have the same return on investment in a contracting consulting services marketplace. The main advantages of these changes are that they can be made fairly quickly and won't impact company morale as significantly as reducing headcount would. That said, the underlying motivation for these changes still need to be well communicated to the whole company so people understand that these are not arbitrary or permanent changes.

Good suggestion. Although it may not be the largest source of cost containment, noncritical expenses not directly related to client service and new customer acquisition/sales are the kind of low-hanging fruit that a company can eliminate as a means of reducing operating expenses during difficult economic times.

Interviewer: Okay, I can see that this suggestion might be a good source of cost savings in the near term. Are there other things the COO could focus on doing?

Time to go further and explore some additional avenues.

Nailing the Case

Candidate: Yes, the other main source of expenses that I mentioned earlier had to do with the salaries and other expenses related to full-time employees. This is a much trickier issue, since letting employees go during tough times does save you money but also carries up-front incremental expenses in the form of severance payments. If, however, the COO believes that the downturn in revenues and demand for her company's services is going to be prolonged, reducing headcount makes sense so that the company can avoid having to bear the costs of under-utilized resources. This also assumes that the company's employees aren't unionized or employed under long-term contracts—both of which will prevent the ability to change the size of the labor force in the short term.

While firing employees does save money, it also brings with it new expenses. These new expenses must be considered on balance when evaluating the total impact of this kind of change on overall expenses.

Interviewer: Letting employees go could save the company significant money, assuming that the overall business is contracting. The COO has actually been considering this drastic step, as she is pretty bearish on the economy and on the overall demand for her company's services in the near as well as the longer term. If the COO accepted this recommendation, what else would you want to suggest she consider before directing her managers to reduce their headcounts?

Candidate: First, I would counsel her to conduct a solid analysis and business case for the need to reduce her staffing and be very focused about where and how she would carry it out. Since this is such a drastic and emotional step for the company, I would counsel her to avoid using an across-the-board reduction in headcount and instead in a targeted manner gauge where the reductions in headcount will be most appropriate—she would need to work with the different P&L or business division managers who know best what their employee needs will be to deliver on the company's existing client needs and service commitments.

Second, I would suggest she very clearly communicate the headcount reduction plan to the CFO and investor relations team so that they can manage Wall Street's understanding of why and when this step is happening. The last thing you want is to have the money managers who rate the company's stock price to overly penalize the company when the staff reductions become public knowledge. Third, I would advise her to be open about the task at hand to all of the internal stakeholders. In this way, the cost-containment activities will not seem like an arbitrary directive coming down from on high, but instead will be clearly connected to the reality of a downturn in the marketplace that necessitates such changes. Finally, I would counsel her to test the wisdom of making such drastic changes with other senior executives before carrying out the plan. I believe that the COO's internal reviews and communications on the decision will be vital in carrying this out in an effective manner.

Good job. Bonus points for showing a more savvy understanding around the challenges of reducing employee expenses through layoffs. Firing is a highly charged and difficult process for most companies—not only will it negatively impact morale, but it will also create new challenges for managers to have to handle. As well, it will potentially send very visible, public signals to the marketplace about the company's opinion of its business prospects in the long term.

Interviewer: Your suggestions make sense. Good job. Thanks for sharing your ideas.

Case 8

Your client is the vice president of global sourcing for a U.S. footwear company. The company once owned seven manufacturing plants in the United States but now only owns a single plant. The client has brought you in to determine whether to close the final plant. What types of questions would you ask to assist the client in making the right decision?

This is a relatively straightforward operations case that discusses the timely business subjects of offshore manufacturing and outsourcing. Most interviewers will expect the candidate to be reasonably well versed in the basic tradeoffs between domestic versus international sourcing and manufacturing.

Bad Answers

- The move towards global sourcing is always justified because the costs will be lower. If the client has closed seven plants, it probably makes sense to close this one as well to reduce costs, improve profits, and satisfy shareholders.

- I am getting sick of companies moving offshore and taking away jobs from American workers. It's companies like these that are responsible for the loss in manufacturing jobs.
  It's stating the obvious, but we'll do it anyway: Make sure not to make your political views blatantly evident in your interviews. It can do nothing but harm your chances of getting hired. That said, keep your emotional opinions about critical issues in check and focus on the task at hand: tackling a case interview in a logical and structured manner. Your interviewer will be looking equally at the manner in which you address the case and at the methodology you use to crack it.

Good Answer

Candidate: Interesting question—and a timely one. I've read a lot about companies facing this same dilemma over the last year. Let me first ask a little more about the company: What types of shoes does it make? What customer segment, or segments, does it target? What are its price points? And what channels does it compete in?

Interviewer: The client targets women exclusively and provides a wide product offering, from work shoes to dressier, fashion-based shoes. Its price points vary—from $50 all the way up to $400. And it owns its own distribution channel, with small stores across the country. It does not have any international distribution.

Candidate: One or two more questions before I start testing some hypotheses: You mentioned that seven plants have been closed. What was the reason that the plants closed, and where did the production move to?

Interviewer: The plants were closed because the client determined that costs were too high. Most of the sourcing has since moved to Asia.

Candidate: Unfortunate, but not surprising. So the client makes a wide range of shoes, some basic, some more fashionable, but still targeted towards the same consumer, who appears to be a working woman. Digging a little deeper, I'm going to assume that the key purchase drivers for the target's work shoes are comfort, price, and a baseline level of fashion. That said, the target will splurge for her dressier, more fashion-based shoes. Is this correct?

Interviewer: It is, but why are you making these assumptions?

Though the candidate may (and in this case does) have very legitimate reasons for going down this path, she has not explained up front how and why she is taking this slant and has therefore lost the interviewer. Not a big deal, but she will need to quickly articulate the rationale for her line of assumptions.

Candidate: The reason I'm asking is because the client may need to employ a different service model for the fashion market than for the work market. For example, it may require different lead times, different manufacturing expertise, or different materials. And this may imply a different sourcing strategy.

Good recovery. A better tactic would have been to share this thought process before discussing the purchase drivers with the interviewer.

Interviewer: I see. Tell me more about what you mean by lead times and why the different markets might require varying lead times.

Candidate: I'm defining lead times as the time it takes the company to design a shoe until the time it is on the shelf. Lead times may be different based on the product segment precisely because of each shoe's varying shelf life. Fashion-based products only have a short window of time in which they are—for lack of a better word—in fashion, while the work shoes are likely to be more consistent year after year.

Interviewer: And what does this mean for our client?

The interviewer is pressing the candidate to turn her insight into implications for the client. Whenever possible, try to do this before the interviewer explicitly asks for them.

Candidate: For fashion products, the client needs to get the product on the shelf expeditiously, and may not be able to wait for the long lead times from Asia. Having a plant in the United States would allow the client to respond to market trends expediently and quickly stock its stores with fashionable shoes. And, given that the consumer is willing to pay a little more for her dressier shoes, the tradeoff between a higher priced shoe and the higher cost structure from a domestic plant might be worth it. In fact, if the client were the only plant to have an American plant, perhaps this could be a competitive advantage.

The candidate outlines the client implications succinctly, with an extra point about competitive advantage thrown in at the end. Some interviewers may not react kindly to this bonus information, because the competitive set has been mentioned; others may be impressed by the candidate's ability to push the analysis to the next level.

Interviewer: You've nailed one of the key issues. The client has kept the last plant in order to service the needs of its more fashion-conscious consumer, who demands a product that is "trend-right." All of the work shoe products have been moved overseas. Now let's see if we can quantify the tradeoff you talked about and make a recommendation. The client has recently put together some analysis saying that it can make the same fashion shoes in Asia for 20 percent less, but that this will add 6 weeks to the lead time. How would you analyze these results?

Candidate: So we're trading off a 20 percent reduction in costs versus 6 weeks of lead time. The answer will lie in how important those 6 weeks are. This brings us into the competitive nature of the market. Is the client now leading the market in getting its fashion product to market? And is its brand equity based on an avant-garde product line?

The candidate now formally introduces another C: competitors. She also asks more about the company, and where its equity with consumers lies.

Interviewer: Over the last couple of seasons, the client has introduced the "It" shoe for the women's fashion market; this has significantly driven up sales in this segment. Women have waited in lines that have stretched over city blocks in order to buy the shoes, which have retailed for $400, up from $250 in the years before.

This interviewer must have recently sold a big project, because this is a real giveaway.

Candidate: Well, in that case, it wouldn't seem to make a lot of sense to lose the brand equity, the price premium, and the sales for a 20 percent cost differential.

Interviewer: How would you calculate the break-even point?

The interviewer, realizing he was being too nice, now throws the candidate one last zinger.

Candidate: I would determine the average profitability under the two scenarios. The base case would involve producing the shoes in the United States with the higher cost structure. The other case would be producing the shoes in Asia but losing 6 weeks. I would assume that both the price point and the total sales would be lower under the second scenario, because the client is giving up its positioning as the maker of the "It" shoe. Then you would need to determine whether the lower cost structure would make up for it.

Interviewer: So if I told you that the average margin on the "It" shoe for the past two seasons was 25 percent, how far could the price fall before the lower cost structure would make sense?

Well, maybe one more zinger.

Candidate: If the shoes have sold for $400, this means that the cost was $300. Moving to Asia would mean production costs of $240. To make the same dollar profitability per shoe, the price could be $340. Ultimately, then, the question is whether waiting those 6 weeks will cut into the price by $60 at retail.

Interviewer: That's the question. Thanks for talking this out with me.

Business Strategy Questions

Case 9

Your client is a large passenger cruise line company. It's considering whether to invest $250 million in a new, 1,500-person passenger ship. The CEO of the company has recently declared publicly that he hopes to deliver 10 percent returns on all major investments. Help the client determine if this is a good investment.

The fact that this question is peppered with numbers implies that the interviewer is looking for a quantitative answer.

Bad Answer

Let's see . . . $250 million investment, 10 percent return. This means that you need to make $25 million on the investment. Let's say that the CEO needs 10 percent return over 10 years, that's $2.5 million a year. That's about $1,500 in profit per passenger. That sounds like a pretty hefty profit per passenger, so I don't think it's a good investment.

The candidate has certainly shown an ability to make assumptions, but he wildly over-simplifies the case and, in doing so, loses serious credibility.

Good Answer

Candidate: Interesting question. I can already tell there's going to be quite a bit of math involved here, so would you mind if I took a couple of minutes to write some things down?

Interviewer: No problem. Take your time.

There is no down side to taking a few minutes (though no longer) to gather your thoughts. Write down all of the factors to consider. In this case, the candidate will want to consider (among other things) the price per passenger, margins, cost structure, capacity utilization, and number of trips per year. Make sure you organize these types of things in a logical fashion so that your structure becomes apparent to the interviewer.

Candidate: Okay. Thanks for your patience. I have a clarifying question to start off with: When you say that the CEO needs a 10 percent return on investment, this means the total return needs to be $250 million plus 10 percent, or $275 million. Does the CEO have a timeframe for this payback?

A good start. The interviewer might be expecting the MBA student to calculate a return based on the time value of money (therefore the discounted return would be higher than $275 million in today's dollars, factoring in the client's cost of capital).

Interviewer: The CEO is looking at a 5-year payback period.

Candidate: So $275 million over 5 years is equivalent to $55 million in profit per year from the vessel. For simplicity's sake, can we make it $50 million a year?

Don't worry if you can't do this in your head. Do the math on a piece of paper. Also, it's completely acceptable to make the numbers you're working with very simple. The candidate has shown a facility with math, which is the most important skill to demonstrate on this case.

Interviewer: No problem. So what we've determined is that the ship has to generate $50 million in income per year in order to break even.

Candidate: Let's start out with the revenue side of the equation, then move to costs. Revenue is going to be a function of price and volume. Volume is going to be equal to the number of passengers multiplied by the number of trips per year. So, for example, if the ship does ten trips per year, its total capacity is 15,000 passengers. How many trips does a ship like this typically take in a year?

The candidate has broken down the revenue portion of the income statement logically and asked a very targeted question that will allow her to continue her diagnosis.

Interviewer: A vessel like this does about 40 trips per year—40 week-long cruises with about 12 weeks for maintenance and repositioning (which means moving from one vacation spot, such as the Caribbean, to another vacation spot, such as Alaska).

Candidate: So this means that the total number of potential passengers is 40 X 1,500, or 60,000. However, the ship is not always going to be full, so the actual load is going to be less than 60,000. Let's assume that, on average, the boat is 75 percent full; this means the actual number of passengers is 60,000 X 75 percent.

This is not easy math to do in your head. Again, take your time and do the math on a piece of paper.

Candidate: 60,000 X 75 percent = 45,000.

Interviewer: Why did you choose 75 percent as your capacity figure?

Interviewers will often challenge you on your assumptions to make sure they are backed by sound business logic.

Candidate: My logic was this: At key times, for example during the holiday season and the summer, the boat is likely to be at full capacity with people taking their vacations. Let's say that this covers about one-third of the year. At other times—during the off-season—the boat is not going to be full; let's say it will be at about 60 percent capacity. The weighted average is about 75 percent.

Interviewer: Sounds like good logic to me. So now what do we do with this 45,000 figure?

Satisfied with the response, the interviewer wants to move on.

Candidate: We need to multiply it by a price per passenger figure to get total revenue. I haven't gone on a cruise lately, so let me ask what's included in the price in order to get a sense of what the fee might be.

Interviewer: The price includes all lodging, food and beverage (except for alcohol), and onboard entertainment activities such as movies, shows, and dancing.

Candidate: Got it. Since I imagine that different cruises target different consumer segments—and charge different prices—I'm going to need to know what type of cruise ship this is.

The candidate is seeking a key piece of information. Always remember to inquire about the customer.

Interviewer: This is a high-end cruise ship, targeting an upper-income bracket.

Candidate: To come up with an estimate, I'm going to use a benchmark, which is how much a consumer in this demographic might spend for a week's lodging and food on a noncruise vacation.

The candidate is now showing her logic before presenting a conclusion. This marks a shift in the approach she used earlier in the interview (when she used the 75 percent figure without giving any background). The interviewer will note this as a positive change made by the candidate.

Candidate: Let's say that this consumer, while on vacation, is accustomed to paying $200 per night and spending $50 per person per day on food, and $50 per person on entertainment. So this means the consumer is paying $300 per person per day, or $2,100 per person per week. It's conceivable that the cruise could then charge in the $2,000 per person range.

The candidate makes a subtle error in judgment. See if you can determine what it is before you proceed.

Interviewer: Actually, this isn't totally accurate. How would it change your math if I were to tell you that the typical consumer for a high-end cruise is an older couple who, of course, shares a room?

The interviewer is letting the candidate correct her own error. As a general rule, an interviewer will not ding a small mistake in a long—and quantitative—case, as long as the candidate recognizes the error, corrects it, and doesn't show signs of frustration.

Candidate: Oops, my mistake. I assumed the consumer was a single person traveling, not a couple. This means the hotel costs need to be divided by two in order to get to a per person number. So, the number would be more like $200 per person per day, or $1,400 per week.

Good recovery.

Interviewer: Do you think the $1,400 per week is reasonable? What factors might increase or decrease the price relative to a "plan your own vacation"?

Candidate: I think you'd be able to charge a small premium on a cruise relative to a "plan your own vacation." On a cruise, everything is very accessible, and all services are taken care of in advance. Convenience is likely of great value to the older consumer. So, to make the math easy, let's assume that a cruise can charge a $100 premium, so the price per person per week would be $1,500. If you multiply this by the 45,000, you get roughly $70 million in annual revenue.

The candidate has wrapped up the revenue portion of the equation. Even if this number is wildly off—which it very well may be!—the interviewer is going to be far less concerned with the final answer than with the logic involved in getting there.

Interviewer: Okay. So, getting back to our initial analysis, you said that the ship would have to generate about $50 million per year in order to break even. Given the revenue analysis you just did, do you think this is possible?

Candidate: This would imply that the cost of maintaining the vessel is only $20 million per year. Stated another way, the margins in this business would need to be really favorable to generate $50 million in income on only $70 million in revenue. I don't know a lot about the specific economics, but this seems really high relative to most industries.

The candidate is using sound business judgment to assess the situation, speaking in terms of margin, and comparing the very high margin required to justify this investment against other industries.

Interviewer: You're right. The margins do seem too high. Do you have any ideas as to how the cruise could increase its revenue stream in order to justify the investment?

Candidate: One option, of course, would be to increase the price, but this might force many of the consumers to substitute other types of vacations for cruises. Other ways might include providing revenue-enhancing options on the boat, such as classes, a casino, skeet shooting, special restaurants where guests would be asked to pay additional fees. You also mentioned that the boat does quite a bit of repositioning. Perhaps the client could increase the number of overall paying passengers if it offered discounted fares during these times as well. But, still, I don't see how the client can justify this investment.

The candidate has come up with several creative solutions and has also taken the next step: assessing the impact of these possibilities on the economics.

Interviewer: Good job! I bet you never thought you'd be discussing skeet shooting during a case interview.

Case 10

Your client is a large regional grocery store player. Most of its stores are located in typical, suburban strip mall-type locations. But that market is almost completely saturated and competition in the grocery industry is fierce, especially with Wal-Mart aggressively expanding its supercenters. The client is looking for new growth options. One idea in front of the CEO is to expand into inner-city communities that have typically been underserved by retailers in general. How might you evaluate this strategic option?

This is a typical, broad-based, and meaty strategy question. It would be appropriate for undergrads or grad students. For an undergrad, this would be a very typical case question, since it deals with a subject—grocery stores—that should be familiar to virtually everyone.

Bad Answers

- I don't know anything about the inner city except for what I've seen in movies. I don't know any poor people. Can I have a different question please?

  Wrong answer on a few levels! Not only does the candidate sound like a snob, he's also committed the cardinal sin of case interviews: punting on a question without making any discernible effort to come up with a solution. And he's made a snap judgment about the customer base—which, as you'll see, is not necessarily the right one.

- It would be dumb to go there. People in the inner city are poor and therefore can't buy enough of your stuff. And you don't want anything to do with that market. Poor people just need to work harder and get jobs. This would be like corporate welfare.

  Whoa! It's generally a good idea to avoid aggressive political statements in case interviews. Not to mention the fact that the candidate has still ignored any relevant facts that might pertain to the case.

- Well, people do have to eat, so it might work. But there's too much crime, and it would be hard to get the trucks in there, so it just wouldn't be worth the hassle. I'd have to say, don't do it.

  Slow down! There are some decent initial points here and they will certainly merit some additional exploration. But the candidate has jumped right to a conclusion, he's got no framework, and he hasn't even given himself a chance to shine.

Good Answer

Candidate: Wow. Interesting issue. That's a lot to think about. Let me ask a question before I dive into a plan. How exactly are you defining inner city? Is there a specific location you have in mind?

Interviewer: Very good question. There are a number of ways to think about inner-city neighborhoods. This is actually an area we spent some time defining for the client. In practice, we are almost always considering a few specific locations, and you can probably picture a few inner city–type locations that are currently not served by a grocery store, but where you could imagine one. For the purposes of this exercise, however, let's think generically about inner-city locations. We can say a few things about them: (1) They are areas in which the median income is significantly lower than that of the metropolitan area as a whole; (2) unemployment is generally higher than in the rest of the region; and (3) there is currently a relative lack of retail options, especially large grocery stores.

It's okay to ask a clarifying question up front. In this case, it was a smart move as it provided the candidate with some valuable information and gave him some time to think. Just don't let your early questions drag on too long or get you distracted from your framework and strategy for dealing with the case.

Candidate: Thanks. That's helpful. There's so much to think about here that I'll try to come up with a clear plan to do so. I'll think out loud while I jot down some notes. I'd like to think about a few things, including (1) the size of the market in terms of both people and income; (2) competition—current ones as well as future potential entrants; and (3) the challenge of doing business in this market, mostly in the area of store operations.

This is fine for a framework. The candidate could probably do a classic "4Cs" with this case if he so desired. Any clear framework will typically do, just so long as you have one.

Interviewer: That sounds good so far. Why don't you start with the size of the market?

Candidate: It's potentially big, right? I'd check out the actual data of course, but can I assume that many people live in these neighborhoods?

Interviewer: Yes, that's a safe assumption. The population in inner-city neighborhoods as we've defined them is quite large. More than 30 million people in the USA live in inner cities, in fact.

Candidate: That's what I thought. So we know the potential market is huge in terms of people. And you've told me that there are few stores serving them now. I'd want to hold off on getting more into the competition until later on, but let's just say that the lack of it initially will be a good thing for us. And it seems to me that everyone has to eat—meaning I'd prefer to place a bet on a grocery store rather than, say, a music store.

Interviewer: Good start. Let's throw a little wrinkle in here now. A consultant is often charged with figuring out good ways to test theories and do research. You said you want to check out the data. How might you go about testing the ideas you've just shared regarding market size?

This type of question occasionally comes up, especially in later rounds when it's already been determined that you can handle such a question. An interviewer will want to see how creative and practical you can be in thinking through how you'll actually do the work. Sometimes you'll even be asked to role play. It doesn't happen often, but keep it in mind.

Candidate: Hmm. Trial by fire for me, today, huh? Okay, here are some ideas. I'd look at census data to get populations and income levels. I'd want to get traffic patterns for cars and buses and see how much traffic other stores are getting in the area.

Interviewer: How would you specifically do that with the traffic patterns?

Candidate: Well, it seems there are specialist firms involved in almost all types of research these days, so we could probably buy that kind of data. But if push comes to shove, we could go out and observe in person for a day.

You can typically buy all kinds of customized research these days. But often "brute force" reconnaissance is the way to go, with junior consultants performing this type of work.

Interviewer: Sounds fine. Let's move on. I'd like to dig more into this market-sizing piece and talk specifically about income levels and whether they matter.

The candidate is getting a direct hint here. He'd be wise to take it. If an interviewer is this specific, she wants you to follow the lead.

Candidate: Well, as I noted before, everyone has to eat, so I'd assume that there'd be some base level of sales you could count on. But we also know that the median income is much lower than those found in typical suburbs; this is a problem. I have to think, though, that there's an advantage being in the city because you've got a lot more people living in a smaller area, what with the taller apartment buildings and such. This has to be positive for a grocery store. From what I know of suburbs, folks will drive 3, 4, 5, or more miles to get to a store. In the city, you'd probably have the same number of customers within a 1-mile radius.

Eureka! This is a key point in the case. In the trade they call it "income density" and you can think of it as dollars per square mile. If the candidate hadn't thought of it himself, the interviewer would probably have prompted him somewhat, perhaps using data, especially since she has a follow-up question. If the candidate were very cagey, he might have mentioned early on that grocery stores have very big fixed costs since they are large and pay lots of rent. Therefore, they often think of their performance in terms of dollars per square foot. This is a good example of a piece of data that you'd know if you'd ever worked in the retail field, and one that you might come up with yourself. And yet you would not be expected to know the terminology.

Interviewer: Good point. Let's test it briefly. Suppose I showed you some limited data:

Store	Cost per Square Foot ($)	Median Household Income ($)	Total $M per Square Mile
Suburb store A	455	75,000	2.7
Suburb store B	639	95,000	3.5
Inner-city store A	812	40,000	5.8
Inner-city store B	711	35,000	4.1

Candidate: Perfect! Just what we needed. So it looks like our theory is correct based on this data. While average income is lower, the *total* dollars to be spent in a given trade area is actually higher in the inner city. In the suburbs, the average dollar per square foot is . . . let's see, let's call it $450 and $650, so we're talking roughly $550. In the city, it's right around $760. That's a considerable difference in favor of the city. And it seems to be coming from the income density you mentioned. In the 'burbs, the density is about 3.1 million per mile while in the city it's more like 5.0 million. I'd want to run a regression against more data, but this feels right so far.

Occasionally you will get a little numbers test in the middle of a case. It will typically be relevant to the case and will often be a market sizing-type question. Sometimes the point is to get to some case insight; other times it can just be a quick test of your math facility and willingness to engage in, rather than shy away from, numbers. In this case, it was a mix of the two. The candidate used round number estimates and drew a quick conclusion. Good for him.

Interviewer: Good. Let's briefly talk about one more issue you think is important.

She's left it open for the candidate, so he can pick his favorite. She said "briefly" and "one more" so the candidate knows they're heading toward the end. Brevity, therefore, is the way to go.

Candidate: Then let's quickly touch on store operations. I'll bet some things would be harder in the city. You'd have to deal with the crime issue, both in terms of theft of goods and the security of the customers. And I think you might have some employee-training issues because the overall education level might be lower. I'd want to interview some successful inner-city store managers and see how they deal with these issues. And you might have differing demands for product mix because you could have different ethnic groups in the city. In my experience, big stores like to carry all of the same stuff. We'd have to learn more here—talk to some store managers. I might want to do a focus group with some inner-city residents to see what kind of products they like to see in their stores.

Interviewer: Good thoughts. And you read my mind on the follow-up tests that you'd do. I like that. This has been a good discussion so far. Let's bring it home to an initial conclusion. Can you summarize and give me a recommendation?

Sometimes an interviewer will request a summary. If that's the case, by all means give it. Other times she won't and the end of the discussion will just sort of hang there. In the latter case, briefly summarize your findings and make some sort of conclusion. Consulting is ultimately about making recommendations to clients—you will look your best if you process the information and turn it into something more real.

Candidate: Sure. Let me summarize some of the "pros":

- Fertile new ground: We need a place to grow and this market is wide open and big.
- An edge over Wal-Mart: It's hard to get its big stores in there.
- Population density: There are more dollars per mile, even if average incomes are lower.

- Rent: This could be lower, but we'd have to explore that more.

- Labor pool: Higher unemployment could mean a benefit for hard-to-fill retail jobs, but we must be aware of potentially higher training costs.

Good list. Nice summation of key points. Note that a couple of the points were not discussed much in the meat of the case. That's okay in a case like this. Be sure to touch on the ones you do discuss.

Candidate: Now on to the "cons":

- Crime or perception of crime: Perception might be worse.

- Labor supply: In inner cities, the labor pool may have less training.

- Income level: Population density argument seems real, but we're still not sure how this will affect the product mix and margins of the store.

- Infrastructure: It could cost more to upgrade site facilities, access, and so on.

- Lack of space: It might be harder to build bigger, prototype stores.

Interviewer: Fine. So where do you come out?

Candidate: Well, there are strong arguments for both sides. But I'd say it feels like the pros outweigh the cons. Even though we're talking broadly about the inner-city market, the reality is that you'll be trying one or two stores at first, so the relative risk won't be as great. If it doesn't work, you can pull the plug. Plus, you won't learn some of the answers unless you try.

Good job. The candidate has made a decision and supported it well. It doesn't matter if it's right or wrong, and in this case, it's pretty much impossible to be right or wrong anyway. The candidate showed savvy by pulling back in on the general nature of the discussion and focusing on the specific reality of the decision.

Interviewer: Super. Good summary. And I'm glad you put a stake in the ground. When we did this project, that's very much what we told the client. They're still working on the first few stores, but early indications are very positive.

Well done. The candidate brought some structure to a wide-ranging case. These types of cases are not easy because there's much to cover and the tendency may be to jump around. The candidate handled the mini-numbers section. He drew on some personal experience, which is always good. (In a case like this, you might be tempted to draw too much on personal or anecdotal experience, since shopping is so common to all of us. Just be aware of this tendency.) The candidate followed prompts well—always a good thing. Remember that interviewers typically base their cases on work that's familiar to them, so they often have a few directions they want you to go. Take their prompts seriously. This was a fun case with real business and societal implications. If you liked this case, you might very well like consulting.

Case 11

You have just joined a sportswear clothing company with a long tradition of making polo-style, short-sleeve shirts and casual button-down, long-sleeve shirts. Let's call this company Eli's. The division within Eli's that you've joined was formed 6 months before your arrival. This new division designs and manufactures shirts for hip, young, fashion-forward urbanites, made in a similar style to those of several other smaller shirt makers who've burst onto the fashion scene in recent years. Your division is losing a significant amount of money, and your manager has assigned you the project to determine what should be done. What do you need to know, and what would you do to assist your new division at Eli's?

This is a case focused on a classic strategy problem—one similar to any number of business strategy problems you would likely face on a typical management consulting project or within many types of manufacturing and marketing organizations in a competitive marketplace. There are one or two pieces of important information that the candidate should be able to infer from the interviewer's description, or set-up, of the case problem. However, most of the information the candidate needs to properly analyze the strategy issues at play here require further probing on the part of the candidate. This case therefore tests the candidate on both her ability to acquire the proper information to identify the nature of the business strategy problem and her ability to develop one or more potential solutions and communicate them as options (rather than answers) for the interviewer to consider. Strive for simplicity with these types of strategy case questions by thinking of them as having two parts: one part information discovery and synthesis, and the other analysis and development of recommendations.

Bad Answers

- Well, I've already identified the main problem: Eli's must have bad shirt designers who just don't know what kids want these days. I would fire all of my designers and hire new ones. Problem solved, profits up and to the right on the graph for next quarter, baby!

This answer is facetious, as no candidate in her right mind would take such a curt and arrogant approach to answering such a potentially complex business problem. However, it's meant to illustrate one key point: In 99 of every 100 strategy case interview situations, you will not have enough information just in the case setup to be able to provide a recommendation. Instead, always consider the many areas you could or would investigate to gather more information before jumping to conclusions or answers to the case problem. Answers like this one demonstrate that the candidate thinks she knows enough to handle any business problem, no matter how foreign the subject matter. Hence, short and quickly considered responses that jump directly to the recommended course of action—without any probing or consideration of alternative strategies to address the problem—are among the worst things you can do in a strategy case interview.

- I'm not so interested in the fashion and retail industries. As my cover letter indicated, I'm really interested in working in finance, so I'm not sure I'd have very good ideas about how to help a company like Eli's—the kind of place I'm never going to work at anyway. Can we talk about an example of a problem that an investment bank might have? I know a lot about how to deal with problems in finance.

  Even if you've indicated a preference for a specific type of functional role, industry affiliation, or the nature of work you'd like to do if hired by the company interviewing you, this is not the time to reinforce what you are and are not interested in doing. The interviewer is not seeking an answer on or insight into how much personal knowledge, research, or interest you have in the fashion industry. Indeed, the candidate's background, previous knowledge of a specific industry, and career interests are all almost entirely irrelevant to a successful performance in the strategy case interview. Instead, these cases allow the interviewer to gain insight into the candidate's general knowledge and application of generic business strategy principles. Do a good job in the interview, get the job offer, and only then talk details with the company about what you'd like to work on when you join them.

- It's probably just that people don't like the new shirts Eli's is designing, or they must be priced too high. Or maybe they're made in the wrong sizes or the color scheme isn't right for the season. Do you have pictures of Eli's shirts and some of the other more stylish shirts that I can look at?

  Interviewers will only rarely have visual aids, graphs, or numbers for what's going right and wrong in the situation with which you are presented. And when they do, they'll provide them to you. So, don't ask. The candidate makes another misstep by using definitive language such as "must" and "isn't right." Let the interviewer use this type of language in describing the problem—those are the facts. The candidate should instead use open, probing language that indicates her mind remains open to many possibilities until she has gained enough information to begin formulating possible recommendations for action; such words include "could," "might be," "perhaps," and so on. Finally, the candidate is already pigeonholing the problem as being one focused on the consumer demand side of things. In so doing, she is closing herself off to the possibility that supply-side or operational problems might be the cause for higher costs and lower potential profits, rather than a drop in demand for Eli's shirts. A strong candidate keeps her options open in the first half of the case, during information discovery and consideration.

Good Answer

Candidate: An interesting situation, and one in which I imagine many new hires are thrown into since companies often like to have fresh ideas and approaches applied in lower-performing divisions. Before I begin thinking about how I might respond to this issue, I need to find out more information. So that I can understand the nature of the marketplace and competition, can you tell me if Eli's competitors in the hip, stylish shirt market are also struggling or losing money?

Good start. The candidate has acknowledged that she will need to learn and consider more information before she is ready to make a recommendation. This is the first key step in any strategy project: getting the data. The candidate has chosen a big picture inquiry to start the investigation and data gathering: an assessment of the health of the overall market demand, using the relative fortunes and performance of other shirt makers as a proxy and directional indicator to see if the market holds any promise for Eli's at all.

Interviewer: Good question. Yes, Eli's competitors in the market for hip, stylish shirts are all doing quite well. They are profitable, popular, and all growing fairly effectively. Only Eli's seems to be having problems making money, despite all of the demand out there for these kinds of shirts.

Good information has been provided here, even more than the candidate was seeking. This is often the case with strategy case interviews; the interviewer will generally guide and provide information to the candidate when it is intelligently and respectfully requested.

Candidate: Okay. Based on the information you've just provided, it sounds like the problem is not on the consumer demand side. It sounds like there's interest and demand for these kinds of shirts and that the market is expanding. There are competitive threats to Eli's offerings, but that's natural in a profitable market. I'd like to know more about the reason Eli's believed it could compete against the smaller designers. Did Eli's hire away a particularly talented designer from a competitor?

Interviewer: Yes, in fact your division has hired several designers away from competitors in the last 6 months, but that hasn't helped. You might want to try something else.

Hmmm. The candidate had a theory, and tested it, but was quickly rebuffed by the interviewer, who basically tells her to avoid wasting any time on the "design and aesthetics" aspect of the case.

Candidate: I just know from my sister, who works at Nordstrom's, that certain styles take off in a particular season and then everyone wants them. Maybe Eli's just hasn't hit the right style of shirt yet and needs to try more designs until one turns into a hit?

Interviewer: That's not it at all. You'll need to think about other things if you want to make any progress.

Yikes. The interviewer remains pretty tough and is communicating very clearly that he thinks the candidate is off-track and should switch course. Remember, there's obviously an element of role play at work here, so don't freak out if you meet a tough interviewer or find yourself hitting on a false assumption or down a blind alley. Clients can be tough too, and the interviewer is likely testing your reaction to difficult situations. Just gracefully accept the redirection and take a different tack.

Candidate: Okay, I'd like to learn more about other potential strengths and weaknesses of Eli's that may be impacting its performance in the marketplace. Does Eli's have efficient production and operations capabilities? Are its existing distribution partners all on board to distribute its new as well as traditional designs? Has this division in Eli's had access to a marketing budget to let the marketplace know that these new shirt designs are being sold?

Interviewer: Good questions. As I mentioned before, Eli's is an established and large, well-known shirt maker. Eli's has a strong and fast production set-up, and all of its distribution partners are stocking the new shirt designs in the right areas of their stores. They are just not selling so far. And yes, Eli's has been marketing its new shirts in a splashy ad campaign running on television and in print.

Good. The interviewer seems to have mellowed out a bit and is sharing a bit of useful information.

Candidate: Okay, that's helpful. So it sounds like the problems are not on the fulfillment and operations side of things, since Eli's is such a mature organization and has some great assets in the form of its distribution partners and marketplace reputation for high quality. I wonder if the problem could be with Eli's marketing campaign—was it too costly or confusing? How are Eli's competitors advertising their products to the marketplace?

Well done. The candidate has implicitly demonstrated a knowledge of the most important framework for evaluating strategic business problems: the SWAT analysis. SWAT stands for strengths, weaknesses, advantages, and threats. The candidate has already learned enough about Eli's threats, has probed somewhat on its weaknesses, and has acknowledged that the interviewer has confirmed numerous strengths and advantages for Eli's. However, the interviewer has not explicitly identified any key weaknesses that could explain Eli's profitability problems in this new division. So, the candidate should probe further to try to discover one or more key additional pieces of information. This is what the candidate has done with her line of questioning about Eli's marketing campaign.

Interviewer: It's interesting you should ask that. In fact, Eli's marketing campaign was very expensive, even compared with several of Eli's more successful competitors. Unfortunately, it hasn't worked to stimulate demand. The target audience just doesn't want to buy Eli's new shirt styles. Why do you ask?

The interviewer didn't divulge much here, except for setting up the conundrum of lots of marketing focus but little demand generation. This usually indicates either off-target marketing or ineffective marketing messaging. The "Why do you ask" from the interviewer may indicate that the candidate is getting warmer.

Candidate: The reason I'm asking is that I'm wondering whether Eli's might have made some tactical errors in marketing the new shirts—for instance, marketing to the wrong target audience using the wrong channels or perhaps using more traditional messaging for the new shirts' benefits that doesn't match up with their real benefits and attributes?

The candidate continues to push on an area that seems promising to her, but without seeming too insistent. This is an effective way to test the waters on a new theory and acquire incremental information and direction from the interviewer, if he's willing to supply it.

Interviewer: It's prudent of you to ask for greater detail about how Eli's is marketing its new line. I can tell you that Eli's used very broad-based television and print ad channels, so you can be sure that its target audience is being reached. And while Eli's did try to spice up its messaging and the images used to promote the new line, it decided to stick with its original brand name for these new shirts—the same brand name it's used to sell its more traditional sport shirts and button-down casual shirt lines.

The interviewer continues to dish out subtle but helpful hints. It seems the candidate is finally getting somewhere.

Candidate: That's interesting and helpful to know. Let me just ask one or two more questions, and then I think I'll have enough to pull together a complete picture of what Eli's new shirt division is facing. Then I can start thinking about potential recommendations to address it. Are Eli's shirts significantly more expensive than those of its competitors? Or are they significantly less expensive?

The candidate is starting to become comfortable with where things are heading. However, just to be sure that she's covered all of the bases, she is probing on one last issue—the issue of price—to determine if simple economics is impacting demand. The candidate was right to preface this additional question by indicating that she's close to being ready to move on to the second part of the interview: the development of potential recommendations to address the problem. If she hadn't, the interviewer might tire of the situation. Collecting some information shows a balanced approach to evaluating many sources of the problem. But endlessly pursuing all manner of information in ever-increasing detail can be overkill and may indicate "analysis paralysis"—that is, the inability to leave the pursuit of new information in order to move on to the more valuable, and ultimately more important, part of a strategy case scenario: synthesis of available information into a plan of action to resolve the problem. In this case, the candidate has shown both the desire to move forward soon as well as the inclination to leave no obvious stones unturned. This is a positive thing, a sign of patience coupled with action on the candidate's part—the right balance of thinking skills for a successful business strategist.

Interviewer: No, price isn't an issue here. Eli's new shirts are somewhat more expensive than its more traditional offerings, but so are those of its competitors. The pricing is appropriate to the more hip, status-conscious consumers of these new shirts. That said, you might be on to something with the marketing approach. What are your thoughts on what the problem might be based on what I've told you so far?

Okay, the interviewer has clearly indicated to the candidate that it's time to synthesize available information and begin developing a solution. The candidate should respond by moving forward quickly.

Candidate: Well, given what you've told me, I have two theories about what the source of the problem might be. My first theory is that Eli's has made a mistake in using the same brand name with these new shirts; this may be putting off its target customer. You implied that buyers of these shirts are paying a premium for a luxury item. Maybe there isn't enough luxury and hipness attached to Eli's brand to justify the higher price. My second theory has to do with the marketing images and messaging: Perhaps Eli's target customer isn't interested in wearing shirts that everyone knows about. It may be that the broad-reach marketing campaigns have backfired by giving the impression that these new shirts are just as common and widely available as its other, more traditional styles. In other words, perhaps these shirts need to appear less widely available and well known and instead appear more exclusive or harder to get in order to appeal to the target audience.

The candidate has put somewhat of a stake in the ground, suggesting two potential theories as to why these new products aren't selling as well as competitors' offerings. If one or both of these theories is correct, then the candidate should be thinking about how to address it.

Interviewer: Good thinking. In fact, most candidates I talk to about this case guess a variation on either one or the other of these problems and go straight to a recommendation from there. But you were right on both counts: Eli's problems are both with its brand choice and with its choice of an overly broad marketing campaign. What would you suggest this division do to address these issues and get Eli's new shirt division on the road to success?

Candidate: I have a few ideas. I'll present them separately so that they match up to the different problems Eli's is facing. With regard to the Eli's brand, I don't believe it would be in the company's best interest to try to shift its core brand identity to match up more closely with the hip, stylish, fashion-forward identity desired by the target audience for these new shirts. I'm assuming that Eli's traditional shirts are still the cash cow of its business. As such, Eli's wouldn't want to do anything to potentially threaten or erode this revenue stream. Therefore, I'd recommend that Eli's consider using a new brand to sell its new shirts—a brand that's sufficiently different from the core brand. Eli's can create a new, more appropriate brand identity from the ground up, one that's more appealing to the hipper, status-conscious target audience.

Interviewer: Interesting idea. However, starting a new brand for this new division is a costly endeavor. Do you have any other ideas on how Eli's might accomplish this goal?

The interviewer is probing the candidate now, trying to determine if she has enough breadth of business strategy knowledge to consider multiple potential recommendations or solutions to the same strategy problem. A successful candidate will present at least one or two alternative approaches to address the problem. However, if the candidate cannot think of any additional potential solutions, then she should indicate that she needs a little more time to consider other options and move on to addressing problem number two (rather than ignoring the request or suggesting in any way that there are no alternatives to the recommendation she has already supplied—a move that would be very bad and close-minded indeed).

Candidate: Well, now that I think about it, I might recommend one other way to address the brand problem Eli's is having with its new shirts: It could acquire one of its successful competitors in the fashion-forward shirt industry and continue marketing shirts under this established, and hip, brand.

Interviewer: An interesting alternative. You're right. Eli's is facing a classic "make vs. buy" decision; it has to decide whether a new brand for its new shirt line is the way to go. Well done. Those are enough ways to address the problem.

How about your recommendation about the marketing campaign failing in its first incarnation?

The interviewer is indicating that he's just about satisfied with the course this case interview has run and just wants to hear a little more out of the candidate before concluding. When you hear these kinds of leading indicators—that the interviewer is short on time and about ready to wrap up—you should respect these clues and move to closure. Even if you're excited with new ideas and have lots of potential additional recommendations, you should wrap it up. Again, the case interview is as much about how the candidate handles the situation and reacts to the direction provided by the interviewer as it is about what the candidate says and thinks—just as the successful practice of business involves a combination of good thinking and tact when it involves executives or clients.

Candidate: I'll be mindful of our time, since we've spoken at length today about this particular case, and I'll wrap up quickly with one recommendation for how Eli's could address its marketing missteps—though I could develop a few alternatives if I had more time. My initial recommendation would be for Eli's to learn from the successes of its competitors and in some respects mimic the marketing approaches they're using to convince the same target audience of its value. If Eli's can adapt its marketing images, messages, techniques, and channels to more closely map to those being used by its competitors, Eli's would most likely see a better response from its target audience. As well, Eli's would get a better return on its marketing investment by being more tactical and focused in its marketing expenditures.

Well done. The candidate closed quickly while still indicating that she has the flexibility and skills to be able to consider other options if time permitted. This is a successful navigation and effective closing to the case, acknowledging the nuances and complexity of the problems that Eli's faces. Complex business problems rarely have singular or simple solutions.

Case 12

Your client is a major sports shoe manufacturer. It has been watching the growth in skateboarding-type shoes in recent years and is wondering whether to start producing these shoes and add them to the existing line. What would you recommend?

This is a common new markets/expansion strategy question. In such a scenario, the candidate's task is tiered—first, he must evaluate if the new market has enough potential and longevity for the client to enter it; and second, the candidate must determine whether the correct strategy is to "make" or "buy."

Bad Answer

Candidate: Those things are such a fad. Skateboarding is kind of a pop-culture thing that happens to be hot right now, but I'm sure it will cool off as soon as the alternative types catch on to something new. I'd advise against making a new shoe that's going to be "out" pretty soon.

How does the candidate know where the market for skateboarding shoes is headed without investigating it first?

Interviewer: Do you have any personal information or experience that tells you that the skateboarding shoe market is going to cool off soon?

The candidate is getting a small opening to try to salvage the chance to enter the case and move it forward.

Candidate: Well, I have a younger brother who was really into skateboarding, but lately he seems to be a lot more interested in listening to music. Also, one of the guys he used to skateboard with doesn't board anymore either. So I can just see the trend starting to wear off.

Wow. That's a great recovery. (Note dripping sarcasm, please.) A sample set of two to determine the direction of a global market that a Fortune 500 company is interested in pursuing. This candidate is going to have plenty more time to study the youth market when he goes to work for one of the stores at the mall after graduation.

Good Answer

Candidate: This is an interesting one. I can't say I'm too familiar with skateboarding personally, but I'm sure I can ask some questions along the way to sort through the issues. Before I start thinking about how the client would consider entering this market with one or more new products, I'd like to ask a few questions to determine if the market is worth entering. Can you tell me whether the client has done a market analysis and made a definite decision yet about whether it wants to enter?

Good start. The candidate has clearly spelled out his approach to the case and has started with the big picture. If the interviewer wants to, she can push the candidate by saying no—thus, forcing the candidate to do the work of evaluating the market.

Interviewer: Good question. Some candidates just assume that the client is ready to act; this isn't always the case. In this case, you can assume that the client has done extensive research and determined that this market has legs.

Great. The candidate got what he needed.

Candidate: Thank you. That's helpful. So I'll assume that the client is really trying to determine how to enter the market for skateboard shoes. The first thing I'd like to know is how quickly the client is interested in entering?

The data hunt continues.

Interviewer: Obviously faster is better, as is the case with any new market that's expanding. But the company is willing to wait if necessary, to enter in the right way.

No information is offered here. If the interviewer had indicated that the client was ready to enter quickly, then that might point the direction in favor of buying an incumbent player already in the market. However, the candidate will have to drive forward without much direction—not an uncommon occurrence in these types of case interviews.

Candidate: Let me clarify. I was trying to learn if the client was interested in moving very quickly, in which case buying an existing market player might be a preferable entry strategy; sometimes it's more favorable to buy an existing product, brand, and manufacturing operation to get into a market quickly than to try to build from scratch. However, I'll take a look at a few more relevant issues before making my recommendation.

The candidate does a good job of explaining his thinking so that at least the interviewer can get some insight into why he asked the question.

Interviewer: Okay. . . . Continue.

Candidate: First, I'd like to know whether the client is confident in its designers and their ability to design a shoe that will compete well against existing competitors' skateboarding shoes. The look of a shoe is such an important factor in sneaker shoe marketing these days. Also, I'd like to know whether the client has excess capacity in its production and operations as this would allow it to introduce one or more new shoes into its lines.

The candidate identifies two key steps in the production process: research and design, and production. By exploring these two areas, he can get a sense for whether "make" is a strong option for the shoe company.

Interviewer: In fact, while the client has strong internal design resources for its existing shoe lines, it doesn't have in-house design resources that are knowledgeable about the skateboarding market. However, the client's production capacity is very flexible and could accommodate ramping up several new lines.

Candidate: Interesting. Can you tell me a little about the existing products in the marketplace? Is it the design and brand or the features and details that have led to market leadership so far?

Interviewer: It's a combination of brand and "coolness" plus features that the top brands in the market for skateboard shoes share. But based on the client's research, it appears that the brand association of the shoes is the most important driver for success. Endorsement by leading skateboarders—their association with the brand—is a key element required to create this cachet.

Good information. The candidate will want to analyze this new information to figure out what's actionable and what's not.

Candidate: Interesting. I wonder if there are any skateboarders who aren't currently endorsing shoes, or who are unhappy with the brand they're backing?

Interviewer: There aren't any popular skateboarders who don't already have a shoe associated with them. In fact, three or four of the top skateboarders are all affiliated with one skateboard shoe brand called Snaps. Another leading brand, LaTerry, sponsors two of the top skateboarders. Another much smaller brand called Lucky's is starting to gain some traction and has garnered attention with the recent airing of a popular rock band's video, which copied some of the ads it ran in a skating magazine.

The interviewer appears to be validating much of the candidate's approach, and offering some helpful hints.

Candidate: Interesting. Are any other major shoe manufacturers already in this market? And if so, have any of them purchased either Snaps or LaTerry and kept them as a separate brand?

The candidate has tipped his hand about the possibility of buying an incumbent as a means of entering the market.

Interviewer: Reebok approached Snaps last year about an acquisition but the client heard through the grapevine that Snaps didn't want to sell. Why do you ask?

Candidate: From what I've heard so far, I'm leaning towards a recommendation that the client consider buying a smaller but growing brand in the skateboard shoe market. This offers the advantage of acquiring a brand with existing sponsors and brand presence, and the potential to quickly expand the line by utilizing the client's excess production capacity. The designers they acquire would be able to experiment and come up with interesting new designs more quickly than the client's in-house designers—those whom you say aren't in touch with this particular market. In this case, I'd recommend that the client first consider talking with LaTerry or another smaller brand that hasn't had a negative experience with a potential corporate acquirer like Snaps has had with Reebok.

The candidate has developed what appears to be a workable recommendation. But the candidate should be ready for the interviewer to press further just in case a few more details require further attention as well as to validate the recommendation's practicality.

Interviewer: That seems reasonable. But before making your final recommendation, would you have the client take into account any potential roadblocks or difficult issues?

Candidate: Good question. Yes, I would. First, I would want to do the research to understand brands three, four, and five—ranked behind Snaps and LaTerry—as well as other brands in the market to see if there are any obvious candidates for acquisition. I would primarily want to look at brands that are on an upward trend but are limited by production and distribution—so that my client could grow the new brand quickly. Second, I'd recommend that the client retain the existing brand following acquisition. In fact, I'd recommend that the client consider keeping the acquisition as quiet as possible. In some cases, a clothing brand's appeal to younger and more fashion-conscious consumers is aided by an association with smaller, more experimental companies. The client probably wouldn't want to dilute the brand association built up by the smaller company in this rather niche market by rebranding it. Rather, it would want to retain the existing brand and just expand in a quiet way the available product offerings to reach more price points and styles. Finally, I would recommend that the client use contracts or financial incentives to ensure that the smaller company's marketing and design managers are motivated to stay on board after the acquisition. Since the brand development and design are key assets needed to successfully sell these types of sneakers, and the client presently lacks these assets, it would be a waste of money and time if they were to depart right away. If we could find an acquisition candidate whose key employees were happy to be acquired, then it would ensure that the assets of the smaller company could be married to the production and distribution assets of the larger company for a winning entry into this market.

The candidate makes a knowledgeable defense of his proposed market-entry strategy by listing the key supporting actions or considerations that the client would also need to address in order for the recommendation to work. Undoubtedly, other key considerations need to be taken care of before the client would take action, but a specific and direct list such as the one that the candidate provides here is sufficient proof that the recommendation is well-reasoned and defensible. If all of the pieces of the strategy puzzle—the strengths, weaknesses, assets, and threats in the client's strategic situation—have been addressed, then the candidate is on solid ground.

Interviewer: That sounds like a good list of initial considerations were the client to accept your recommendation to acquire a small existing company as a strategy for entering this growing market. Thanks for sharing your thoughts with me.

Good job. Consider this case successfully navigated.

Resume Questions

Case 13

Most people who enter consulting don't make a career out of it. How does consulting fit into your long-range career plans?

This is a different slant on the "Why do you want to get into consulting?" question.

Bad Answer

At this point, I think that consulting is the career for me. It combines interesting questions with constant access to senior-level executives and will allow me to travel to very exotic places.

The interviewer is going write you off as a phony or he'll interpret your response as sarcastic and write you off as a jerk. The Donald would fire you for this answer.

Good Answer

Candidate: The thing I really like about consulting is that it gives me a skill set that's broadly applicable to whatever I want to do next should I choose not to make a long-term career out of consulting. In particular, there are three skills I'd like to develop further in consulting: problem structuring, analytics, and client relations. These skills will serve me well in whatever career path I pursue in the future.

The candidate does a nice job of structuring his response from the outset, demonstrating that a good structure works well for resume questions as well.

Candidate: I've been impressed by consultants' abilities to take a difficult problem and break it down into more manageable pieces. My business-school friends, who came from consulting, can go up to a white board and quickly break down a problem: They will draw a decision tree or write down a list of ten questions that need to be answered in order to address the larger problem.

Interviewer: How do you think these classmates of yours were able to develop these skills?

Candidate: I'm not completely sure, but I'd imagine one of two ways. First, I think there's probably a bit of the osmosis effect going on—being in an environment where people think in a very logical, structured manner would force me to think in that same way. The second reason has more to do with time constraints. Teams work under tight timelines, so there can't be a lot of wasted effort. Therefore it makes sense to spend some time up front structuring the problem to ensure that the team is focusing its effort on the most critical issues.

The candidate shows a solid understanding of the consulting process.

Interviewer: Sounds right to me. You also mentioned analytics. What analytics do you think are most important? And in which areas do you think you have the most to learn?

The interviewer is changing his question slightly to test the candidate's ability to think on her feet.

Candidate: The most important analytics probably revolve around financial statements: understanding the source of the company's profitability and assessing the key performance drivers over the last years. The answers from this analysis will allow you to go deeper. For example, if revenues are falling, I would need to determine the reasons why: Is the reason lower prices or fewer units sold? Or is the category down? Has the client lost market share? An understanding of the financial statements provides a jumping point for all sorts of subsequent analyses.

Notice how the candidate shows some business acumen in her answer. This will score big points.

Interviewer: And how much experience do you have reading and interpreting financial statements?

Candidate: Truth be told, I have a lot more experience with income statements than I do with cash flow or balance sheets. When I was a product manager, I was responsible for my own P&L. As such, I became very familiar with interpreting results because that's how my performance was measured. At my former company, the balance sheet and cash flow statements were managed at the corporate level.

The candidate is very frank with her answer, but shows that she does have deep experience with one type of financial statement. As a general rule, consultants primarily deal with issues related to the income statement.

Interviewer: The final skill you mentioned had to do with client relations. What do you mean by that?

Candidate: What I mean by client relations is the ability to be poised and articulate in front of senior client audiences. They are paying a lot of money for answers to very difficult questions, and want the answers delivered in a professional way.

Interviewer: Just to manage your expectations, oftentimes only the senior partner at our firm will present to the most senior client. The rest of the team will interact with the client on a lower level. As you know, some cases require a lot of time at the client site. How does this change your answer?

Another opportunity for some quick thinking.

Candidate: I view this as a growth opportunity as well. I've been told that consultants have the chance to lead dedicated client teams and therefore hone their management skills. I think I'm ready for such a challenge. When I was a project manager, I managed a team of three. So I guess, in summary, I look forward to interacting with clients at all levels of the organization.

Nice job. The candidate has successfully avoided giving the interviewer the impression that she only wants senior client interaction and has also conveyed that she has some experience managing others.

Interviewer: Thank you for your time.

Case 14

I see that last summer you worked for a small printing press. Walk me through the decision process that led you to work for this company.

This question is mostly geared to test the candidate's thought process and, similar to most cases, to test for clear, structured thinking.

Bad Answer

The company was small and not really like a consulting firm at all. I'm an English major, and I did it because I was really interested in learning about an industry closely related to my field. I didn't really like it, so that's why I'm interested in consulting.

There is the kernel of a really good answer in here, but the candidate is overly apologetic and denigrates his experience. Most people who go into consulting have never had experience in an industry like consulting. In addition, whatever your prior experiences, do not complain about them: It will just make you come off sounding like a whiner.

Good Answer

Candidate: I'm glad you asked this question, because it actually goes to the heart of why I'm interested in consulting. As an English major, I've struggled with whether to go into the business world or pursue an alternate career, perhaps as a lawyer or a teacher. Last summer, I wanted to test the business waters, but wanted to do something in an industry that was somewhat familiar to me. I looked at a couple of opportunities: working at a major book distributor, with a children's book publisher, and at the small printing press. I finally decided on the small printing press.

The candidate, not surprisingly given his major, is telling a compelling story that helps paint a picture for the interviewer as to why he chose his summer job. He has also cleverly weaved

*in the fact that he had other options—indicating that he must have had some success during
the interview process.*

Interviewer: So why did you go with the printing press specifically?

Candidate: Two reasons, really. One, it was a small company, with only 25 employees and $5 million in revenue. Its size allowed me to gain access to all aspects of the business—from sales and marketing to finance and operations. Second, I connected very well with the owner. We share similar backgrounds, got along very well from the outset, and I felt that he would be a good mentor to me over the summer.

*The candidate has articulated two compelling reasons for selecting the printing press
opportunity. The personal connection bit in particular will resonate with the interviewer.
The importance of teamwork in consulting, and of genuinely liking the people you spend
most of your waking hours with, cannot be overestimated.*

Interviewer: So what types of projects did you work on?

Candidate: I had two main projects. One was to look into opportunities to increase sales by expanding our customer base. Historically, the business's customer base consisted of first-time authors who couldn't get their books published by larger publishing houses and who wanted to distribute them on their own. What I uncovered was an opportunity to partner with large publishing houses to do overruns. Basically these houses would use us as excess capacity.

*The interviewer will be impressed by the concise explanation of the project as well as the
candidate's fluency with business vocabulary.*

Interviewer: Sounds interesting. Is anything happening on this front?

Candidate: Actually, yes. As a result of my work, the company is in talks with a couple of big publishing houses, although I can't tell you which ones.

Confidential work. . . .Exciting!

Interviewer: And what was your second project?

Candidate: The second project was a little more mundane, but equally important. I designed a planning process for the company. Annual strategic and financial planning was very haphazard. For example, no one really had budgets. So I organized a timeline and process for these things to happen in a more structured manner.

Interviewer: Don't think that it's only small printing presses that have backwards or nonexistent planning processes. We do a lot of strategic planning process work with our clients as well. You mentioned that this experience made you more interested in consulting. Why?

Candidate: Basically because it taught me that I like business but I still have a lot to learn. Maybe some day I'll go back and work for this small company. I still talk to the owner every week. But I think that I'll be much more effective if I can develop the broad skill set that consulting offers.

This is kind of a stock answer, but appropriate given the context. The structure and content of this answer will move the candidate on to the next round.

Case 15

I see you used to work in marketing for retail company Z. Did your role and experience there meet your expectations? If so, in what ways was it a good match for your skills? If not, what was the gap and what did you learn from your time in that role?

These types of resume cases, in which an interviewer essentially designs a case around a specific part of your background, are quite common. Your goal should be to convey with clarity and confidence that you have a strong command of the issues facing the company as well as the company's relative success or failure in utilizing your skills. Your primary objective with this kind of question is to demonstrate that you are a thinking employee— in other words, you evaluate your role in the larger organization in which you work and you care about the degree to which you are well suited to your particular job. Your secondary objective is to give the interviewer a sense for what you did, and did not, like about a past work experience so that she can better understand what motivates you. While you shouldn't share company secrets or the like, you can share deeper insights or professional development lessons you learned from your time in a past job experience if appropriate. This shows that you care about and take a thoughtful approach to your career development—a perspective valued by any potential employer.

Bad Answer

To be honest, I was really frustrated and angry while I was working at company Z. I really felt that the management team had its priorities out of whack and it was a hard place to work. I managed to stay 2 years, but it wasn't a great place for growth.

Even if you hold a negative opinion of your former company (you did leave, after all), your interviewer will expect you to have a professional approach to handling the question and subject matter. Confessing that you were extremely frustrated demonstrates professional immaturity and a lack of understanding of the broader context in which you were working. It may also lead the interviewer to believe that you are either overly demanding in your expectations of what a potential employer can deliver or quick-tempered.

Good Answer

Candidate: When I started working at company Z, I was excited about my role on the marketing team. At the time, customer marketing was very important to the senior management team and the internal commitment to the marketing team was apparent. As someone who is passionate about marketing, I was excited about joining an organization where I felt that I could really drive great results in the marketplace in terms of our product and brand awareness. By the end of my first year, we had made a name for our company in the minds of our consumers; our brand was becoming ubiquitous. However, as our customer base grew, senior executives began to examine the company's marketing strategy. What resulted was a gradual shift away from external marketing investments and towards operational improvement and customer price incentives. I found myself in a difficult situation as did other experienced members of the marketing team: As company strategy shifted away from my personal area of expertise, I had to determine how to preserve my passion, interest, and contribution to a company that I had joined primarily based on my marketing and public relations skills.

There's an old saying that everyone's favorite topic of conversation is himself. Resume or past experience questions tee the candidate up perfectly to expound on his assets and skills. This is a valuable opportunity to impress the interviewer. Don't undermine these chances by being bombastic about how great you are, or by going on for too long without involving the interviewer and remembering that this is a conversation—not a speech.

Candidate: In the end, members of the marketing team as well senior managers at the company decided that resources—both people and finances—should be shifted away from direct marketing towards these operational investments. I'm sure you've been in a similar situation at one point in your career, when you could feel the tide shifting and had to be flexible enough to shift the focus of your role.

The candidate has made a savvy move by engaging the interviewer with a positive, rhetorical question. It gives the candidate a chance to take a moment, even as it reaffirms something positive that the interviewer has done in his own career (we all like to have others assume we're smart and flexible). At the same time, it reinforces the fact that the candidate also did something positive in a challenging situation.

Interviewer: I have. No large company is ever static in its strategy or its organization, that's for sure. Tell me what you did to address the strategic changes impacting your role.

Candidate: For some people on the team, in particular those who had been with the company for several years, the apparent shift away from their area of interest and expertise was devastating and frustrating. While I admit that at first I was disappointed in having to pivot away from a role that appeared to be such a perfect fit for me, I also found this to be a great learning experience. I knew the shift away from direct marketing and heavy brand investments was an indication that we'd done our jobs in building broad customer awareness faster and more effectively than anyone thought we could. It was educational to witness—and be a part of—the way strategy and internal departments can shift around as certain business objectives are met. Of course, this shift required that I start exploring other departments to see if I could fill another role in which my skills would be valued even if my job focus changed.

The candidate is demonstrating professional maturity—acknowledging that as company strategy and objectives shift, so do resource requirements. While many people may have difficulty accepting this situation, especially those who care about and work in the impacted departments, rapid change is an inevitable part of the practice of business today. Even though the candidate was personally affected by this change, he recognizes that it was a necessary measure and isn't emotional about what happened. The candidate displays an attitude that is appealing to most interviewers, one that shows he is both proactive in his professional development and flexible enough to understand the reality of an ever-changing business organization.

Candidate: Additionally, even though it impacted me personally, I was proud to be working for a company that really kept the customers' needs front-of-mind—so much so that it shifted internal investments in the best interests of the customer in order to continue to grow loyalty and in turn revenues.

This candidate obviously knows customer retention and understands the future of company Z's business. He also shows his broader understanding of the overall company situation and reasons for this decision. Having effectively communicated the broad perspective, it's time for the candidate to close by focusing on how he handled the situation.

Interviewer: Did you find a new job as your marketing team was dismantled? And how did it go switching roles so abruptly within this company?

Candidate: It was a challenging time. About two-thirds of the marketing team were laid off and asked to leave the company. I realized how hard it is for company morale to bounce back after layoffs. I think what saved me from getting laid off was that I had been proactive about going out into the rest of the company, conducting informational interviews with several other business division managers once I began to see the writing on the wall. Through this process, I was able to find a new role as a product manager on one of the smaller product lines within the company. Switching roles so quickly was a challenge, to be sure, since this new role was more heavily weighted towards strategy than outbound marketing— I was faced with a steep learning curve in the first month or two of shifting roles. However, even though the role was quite different from what I'd expected to be doing when I joined the company, I found that I was learning new and exciting skills related to market research, product development, and pricing strategy. After several more months, I began to realize that a sudden shift in roles is sometimes the fastest—and best—way to learn a valuable new set of business skills. Of course, I've still got more to learn about product management; it's one of the main reasons why I'm interested in a consulting role with your company.

Well done. The candidate gets extra bonus points for connecting the dots between a key learning from a previous job experience and interest in the particular company and role for which he is interviewing today. It helps make the case for why the candidate is an even better fit for the role, and helps convince the interviewer that such a move will advance the candidate's larger career aspirations and professional development objectives.

Interviewer: Thanks for giving me insight into that particular work experience and how you handled the situation. I appreciate your candor about what you managed to learn from what was probably a pretty difficult time. Let's move on to talk about another part of your career.

The candidate shows the ability to handle change and the threat of losing a job with maturity and proactive ingenuity. Dwelling on what he hated or found frustrating about the experience wouldn't have helped anyone. It wouldn't have helped the interviewer learn more about the candidate's qualifications, and it wouldn't have helped the candidate make his case for being a good fit for the job. By focusing primarily on the growth and development aspects of this difficult experience, the candidate shows that even in situations that aren't perfect he can succeed. Many situations in business are less than perfect, but talented candidates find the opportunities inherent in them. Good job!

WETFEET'S INSIDER GUIDE SERIES

JOB SEARCH GUIDES

Getting Your Ideal Internship

Job Hunting A to Z: Landing the Job You Want

Killer Consulting Resumes

Killer Investment Banking Resumes

Killer Resumes & Cover Letters

Negotiating Your Salary & Perks

Networking Works!

INTERVIEW GUIDES

Ace Your Case: Consulting Interviews

Ace Your Case II: 15 More Consulting Cases

Ace Your Case III: Practice Makes Perfect

Ace Your Case IV: The Latest & Greatest

Ace Your Case V: Return to the Case Interview

Ace Your Interview!

Beat the Street: Investment Banking Interviews

Beat the Street II: Investment Banking Interview Practice Guide

CAREER & INDUSTRY GUIDES

Careers in Accounting

Careers in Advertising & Public Relations

Careers in Asset Management & Retail Brokerage

Careers in Biotech & Pharmaceuticals

Careers in Brand Management

Careers in Consumer Products

Careers in Entertainment & Sports

Careers in Human Resources

Careers in Information Technology

Careers in Investment Banking

Careers in Management Consulting

Careers in Manufacturing

Careers in Marketing & Market Research

Careers in Nonprofits & Government

Careers in Real Estate

Careers in Supply Chain Management

Careers in Venture Capital

Consulting for PhDs, Doctors & Lawyers

Industries & Careers for MBAs

Industries & Careers for Undergraduates

COMPANY GUIDES

Accenture

Bain & Company

Boston Consulting Group

Booz Allen Hamilton

Citigroup's Corporate & Investment Bank

Credit Suisse First Boston

Deloitte Consulting

Goldman Sachs Group

J.P. Morgan Chase & Company

Lehman Brothers

McKinsey & Company

Merrill Lynch

Morgan Stanley

25 Top Consulting Firms

Top 20 Biotechnology & Pharmaceuticals Firms

Top 25 Financial Services Firm